BIBLICAL
AUTHORITY

BIBLICAL AUTHORITY

Edited by
Jack Rogers

WORD BOOKS, Publisher   Waco, Texas

First Printing, April 1977
Second Printing, August 1977

Scripture quotations from the Revised Standard Version of the Bible,
copyrighted 1946, 1952, © 1971, 1973 by the Division of Christian
Education of the National Council of the Churches of Christ
in the U.S.A., and used by permission.

Printed in the United States of America
ISBN 0-87680-800-3
Library of Congress catalog card number: 76-56482

CONTENTS

EMBATTLEMENT OR UNDERSTANDING?
A FOREWORD

by Paul Rees

Paul Rees is Vice-President-at-large of World Vision International. He is also a member of the Board of Directors of and Contributing Editor to Christianity Today, *Consulting Editor for* Eternity *magazine, and Associate Editor of* The Herald. *He is author of more than a dozen books, among them* Proclaiming the New Testament: Philippians, Colossians, Philemon; Men of Action in the Book of Acts; Don't Sleep Through the Revolution; *and editor of* Nairobi to Berkeley. *From 1938 to 1958 he served as Pastor of First Covenant Church in Minneapolis, Minnesota, and is now Minister to Ministers for the Billy Graham Crusades. Dr. Rees is a graduate of the University of Southern California, having received the B.A. in 1923 and having been awarded the D.D. in 1944. He is a past president of the National Association of Evangelicals (1952– 54) and has served as director of the Pastors' Conference Ministry (1964–75).*

IN THE SUMMER of 1520 Martin Luther delivered his famous *Address to the Nobility of the German Nation*. Praying that he might be given Joshua's trumpet with which to flatten the walls of the papal Jericho, he blasted the claim that the popes were the lords of Scripture and could not err in faith. Four and a half centuries later the evangelical community is embattled not over the infallibility of the pope, or indeed the infallibility of the Scriptures (in the classical understanding of that phrase) but rather over the infallibility of the word "inerrancy" to describe the total authority and credibility of the Bible in its original form.

One of the easiest ways of going either "pro" or "con" on this issue is to be simplistic. We are tempted to sharpen the either/or gambit to the point where everybody feels he must deliver himself of one of those decisive sentences beginning with, "Nothing could be clearer—" In fact, however, there are a hundred things that to reflective minds could be thrillingly clearer.

Take the deceased B. B. Warfield and the living G. C. Berkouwer as examples of variant viewpoints. Both are men of monumental erudition and profound biblical fealty. Both are committed to the infallibility with which Holy Scripture reflects and reveals God's saving purpose. Yet the flat-out insistence of Warfield on the rigorous use of inerrancy stands in contrast to the reserve with which Berkouwer, equally a confessor of the unique authority of Scripture, treats a word that has less creedal history behind it and more ambiguities associated with it. What is at issue here is not evangelical commitment but evangelical comprehension. There is a difference of understanding as to the way and form in which God has worked to give us the mystery and the majesty, the humility and the authority, of the Word made word—a wonder scarcely less baffling than that of the Word made flesh.

Church history supports the view that times of theological tension and turbulence tend to be times of theological overstatement. Thus when Martin Luther, in the heat of the Reformation struggle, said, "Sin boldly," he could have been taken for a rank antinomian. Heard in context, however, his verbal shocker was intended to underline the all-sufficient merits of Christ our High Priest, requiring neither ecclesiastical indulgences nor absolutions. Yet considered in itself it was a perilous overstatement.

Similarly, take the following from a concerned correspondent who is unhappy with any doctrine of the origin of Scripture other than that of divine dictation:

> They [the writers of Scripture] were given the mind of God in words provided and they were not their own words. In supporting this fact, note that God never speaks from [his] mouth to heart or conscience or intellect, or ever will, but he speaks mouth to mouth. . . . There are 62 references in both Testaments referring to the mouth of the Lord conveying by actual words—HIS WORD.

In an excess of zeal to defend the Bible against an excess of denigration a position is taken—the dictation theory of inspiration—that very few, even among the most conservative of biblical scholars, have ever been willing to espouse. It must be quickly added, however, that many are hard put to show wherein their positions differ *practically* from the dictation formula they repudiate.

In the following pages it will be the reader's privilege to be exposed to the thinking of deeply concerned scholars who are classically evangelical, thoroughly supernaturalistic, and candidly realistic.

They are scholars who stand in the tradition of Augustine, Luther, and Calvin in reverently affirming that the Bible in all its words is the Word of God. They are equally at one with Augustine, Luther, and Calvin in critically examining the human form of words God chose to use in order more fully to understand the divine meaning.

Klaus Runia, a contemporary evangelical theologian, in a paper circulated by the World Evangelical Fellowship, well puts the dual responsibility to Scripture which the contributors to this volume share. Runia declares that "the Bible as the Word of God is infallible in all that it asserts." He then goes on to say:

> The Bible is a Semitic book through and through. On every page it shows its Semitic origin and background, culture and outlook. It would therefore be wrong in principle to approach the Bible with our modern scientific standards and to judge it accordingly. For example, the way of writing history was quite different from what we are used to in our day. Often the Bible writers give no more than approximations. Often they are very schematic in the arranging of their material. But all this does not in any way detract from the infallibility or trustworthiness of the Bible.

Thus the total task of interpreting and confessing the Bible's authority and reliability is by no means as simple as we perpetually try to make it. The Bible's human components and history are as honestly to be reckoned with as its divine origin and preservation. He who cannot acceptingly live with its humanity will always be tempted presumptuously to distort its divinity. After all, God could have *dropped* the Bible ready-made from the skies in 2000 languages or more. He chose not to *drop* it but to *develop* it—over long periods of time and with the help of a lot of human agents. God didn't *bestow* it. He *built* it—piece by piece, event by event, writer by writer. If it was initiated and interpenetrated by heaven—and we believe it was—it was cradled and colored by earth.

Let me touch on several background matters that I think should be kept in mind as one follows the essays that are here brought together:

1. Assertions of biblical inerrancy are made in reference to the original autographs only. None of these is extant, nor is there any reason to believe that we shall ever have access to them.

2. Therefore the inerrancy claimed for the Scriptures does not apply to any version or copy of the Bible that anyone may now be reading or holding in his hand.

3. On that account we should think twice before allowing ourselves to be caught in the dilemma of the often-mentioned "domino theory." As applied to Scripture it means: if you can find one inaccuracy in the Bible you are using, then in one stroke you have made it impossible to say with assurance that anything in the Bible is dependable. It is that brand of reasoning, as well as the mentality that it creates, that should give us pause.

4. It is historically obvious, when the records are studied in depth, that the Christian church, through its confessions and in its leadership, has been exceedingly cautious about formalizing a commitment to inerrancy. The sufficiency, the authority, the infallibility of Scripture as our "rule of faith and practice"? Yes. The total inerrancy that extends to the minutiae of chronology or geography or grammar? No. It is of course maintained by some that the nonappearance of such doctrinalized inerrancy in most of the creeds is simply because such a view was taken for granted. Perhaps. The evidence for it is doubtful.

5. The present renewed discussion of the relationship between inerrancy and the Bible's unique authority threatens to create a serious cleavage in the evangelical community. Although such a split would be as grievous as it would be gratuitous, the build-up for it has been in process for some time. Both Harold Lindsell and Carl Henry have lately referred to the Wenham (Mass.) Conference on Scripture held in 1966. The profile of evangelical invitees was broadly international, interdenominational, and interdisciplinary—from six European countries, Canada, Korea and Australia. What they had in common—some of them specialists on systematic theology, some of them specialists in biblical studies—was a firm evangelical commitment. In organizing such a conference one knows that always some who are invited are

obliged for various reasons to decline. It comes, however, as a surprise to read in Harold Lindsell's *The Battle for the Bible* (p. 32):

> Some of the greatest stalwarts who have consistently defended biblical inerrancy backed out of the conference. They felt that their presence would serve no useful purpose and that little was to be gained by discussing inerrancy with those in attendance whose minds already had been made up against it.

Clearly, Dr. Lindsell, my beloved friend of long years, has feelings that run deep at this point. His gloomy view of that consultation among evangelical brothers may have been shared by some who were in attendance, but certainly not by all. It was a time of candor, of leveling with one another, of facing up to the complexities of the issues that were under discussion.

Is the closed mind, of which Dr. Lindsell writes, to be found in only one corner of the Lord's vineyard? Maybe so. Yet one wonders.

Moreover, is it not right to say that there is a difference between *the* evangelical *attitude* toward the Bible and *an* evangelical's *views* about the Bible? Go back to Warfield and Berkouwer. Their views of how to construe the Bible's matchless revelatory quality and authority are not precisely the same, just as Luther's and Calvin's were not. But their *attitude* toward the Bible is identical—God's Word that shines in our world's darkness, the unerring pointer to the One "who for us men, and for our salvation, came down from heaven . . . was crucified also for us . . . suffered and was buried, and the third day he rose again . . . ascended into heaven, and sitteth on the right hand of the Father. And he shall come again with glory to judge both the quick and the dead, whose kingdom shall have no end."

Hallelujah!

THE CHURCH DOCTRINE
OF BIBLICAL AUTHORITY

by Jack Rogers

Jack Bartlett Rogers is Associate Professor of Theology and Philosophy of Religion at Fuller Theological Seminary in Pasadena, California. Prior to assuming that position in 1971, he served as Assistant Academic Dean and Associate Professor of Religion and Philosophy of Westminster College for several years. While a student, he was awarded the Thomas Jamison Scholarship from Pittsburgh Seminary for study abroad (1959–60) and the Presbyterian Graduate Fellowship by United Presbyterian Church in the U.S.A. for dissertation research (1965–67). In 1973 he was made a Fellow of the Case Study Institute, Cambridge, Massachusetts. Dr. Rogers is author of three previous books (Scripture in the Westminster Confession, Confessions of a Conservative Evangelical, *and* The Family Together [*with Sharon Rogers*]) *and editor-translator of G. C. Berkouwer's* Holy Scripture. *An ordained minister of the United Presbyterian Church in the U.S.A., Dr. Rogers was organizing pastor of Pilgrim Fellowship of the Nederlands Hervormde Kerk (Dutch Reformed Church), in Dordrecht, The Netherlands. Dr. Rogers holds the A.B. in Speech and Philosophy from the University of Nebraska, the B.D. (cum laude) and Th.M. from Pittsburgh Theological Seminary, and the Th.D. from the Free University of Amsterdam.*

EVANGELICALS BELIEVE that the Bible is the authoritative Word of God. On two closely related questions there is significant disagreement: (1) what is the nature of the Bible's authority? and (2) how is that authority known and accepted? This chapter will examine those two questions at several significant points in the history of the church. If we can discover any patterns on which there is consensus in the church, it may give us perspective on some of our contemporary controversies.

For the earliest Christians the biblical writings were linked to the work of the Holy Spirit in bearing witness to the Savior, Jesus Christ.[1] Jesus said regarding the Old Testament writings: "It is they that bear witness to me" (John 5:39). The central purpose of the New Testament writings, according to the Apostle John, was that people might know Christ savingly: "But these are written that you may believe that Jesus is the Christ, the Son of God, and that believing you may have life in his name" (John 20:31).

The first written source of saving knowledge for the early church was the Old Testament. By understanding Jesus as the fulfillment of Messianic prophecy the Old Testament became a Christian book. Most early Christians did not read the Old Testament in Hebrew, but in a Greek translation, the Septuagint. It likely included a group of books which Protestants now exclude called the Apocrypha.[2] The canon, setting the limits of the

17

New Testament, was not officially fixed by the church until late in the fourth century. But all of the materials we have in our New Testament seem to have been in general circulation and acceptance by A.D. 200.[3]

Gradually, the early church had a variety of sources of authority and guidance. It had a body of "teaching"—its history, interpretations of past events and actions, and eventually some creeds. But central for the church was the Bible, containing what had been expressly revealed by God to bring people to salvation and to guide their life of faith. Problems arose when differing individuals or groups used variant texts of Scripture to support their particular "teaching" on certain issues.[4]

Most of the early church was part of a Greek world culture. Christians were influenced by that culture and in turn wished to influence it. They wanted to make Christianity acceptable by putting the Christian message into Greek concepts which educated persons would adopt. Two main schools of thought had been inherited by early Christian culture from the "classical" period of Greek philosophy in the third century before Christ. They were the schools of Plato and Aristotle.

For our purposes we may use the names Platonic and Aristotelian to designate two schools of thought, each of which had significant impact on Christian theology. The Platonic school assumed that the knowledge of great truths, like God as Creator, was born into every person. Knowledge of particular things in this world was known by deduction from those general principles. When applied to theology, the Platonic method assumed that faith preceded and provided a framework to make possible right reasoning.

The Aristotelian school took the opposite view. We are born with blank minds but a capacity for reasoning. All knowledge begins from sense experience of things in the world. We come to general principles by induction from a number of particulars. When applied to theology, the Aristotelian method assumed that reason, based on the evidence of senses must precede and would lead to faith.

Educated Christians in the first centuries of the Christian era were influenced by these philosophical schools and their offshoots. Platonic influences dominated. In part this was because philosophical speculation in the second century A.D. was largely directed to the problem of Providence. Platonists defended Providence. Aristotelians were regarded as atheists because they denied Providence and the immortality of the soul.[5]

Origen

A man who exemplified the blending of Platonic philosophy and biblical thought was Origen of Alexandria (c. A.D. 186–255), the most influential father of the early church. Origen has been called the first great preacher, devotional writer, biblical commentator and systematic theologian of Christianity.[6]

The Bible was authoritative for Origen. The Scriptures were "sacred books," "holy documents,"[7] without which we could have no clear knowledge of God. The Scriptures of the Old and New Testaments had an "inseparable unity."[8] The Bible was harmonious throughout and "supernaturally perfect in every particular."[9]

At the same time, Origen was very conscious of the human character of the holy writings. He knew that the New Testament was not written in the best Greek. But to him, that was unimportant because the revelation did not consist in the words but in the things revealed.[10] Indeed, for Origen, the very reason that human beings could know the revelation of God is that God had "condescended" or "accommodated" himself to our human ways of communicating and understanding. According to Origen:

> He condescends and lowers himself, accommodating himself to our weakness like a school master talking "little language" to his children, like a Father caring for his own children and adopting their ways.[11]

Scripture was the work of a single divine author who adjusted himself to human thought in order that his saving message might be understood.[12]

The great preacher John Chrysostom (A.D. 354–407), who had read some of the work of Origen, also held to the principle of accommodation. Chrysostom said:

> Christ often checked himself for the sake of the weakness of his hearers when he dealt with lofty doctrines and that he usually did not choose words as were in accord with his glory, but rather those which agreed with the capability of men.[13]

Augustine

Augustine (A.D. 354–430) served as a link between the Ancient Church and the Middle Ages. He spoke Latin, not Greek, and was a teacher of rhetoric. His early life is generally well known including the fact that he had dabbled in many religions and philosophies before coming to Christianity.

Preparatory to his conversion to Christianity was a conversion to neo-Platonism. Augustine joined a group of young intellectuals in Milan who were neo-Platonists. With them he heard the preaching of Bishop Ambrose whose sermons were often a synthesis of Scripture and neo-Platonic ideas.[14]

The integration of biblical data and Platonic philosophy can be seen in the famous maxim of Augustine's theological method: "I believe in order that I may understand." The biblical foundation came from the Septuagint translation of Isaiah 7:9: "Unless you believe, you shall not understand." The philosophical foundation was the Platonic concept of innate first principles which enable us to make sense out of particulars. "No one," prayed Augustine, "can call upon Thee without knowing Thee."[15] In "matters of great importance, pertaining to divinity," Augustine declared, "we must first believe before we seek to know."[16]

Almost everyone wants to claim Augustine—Protestants and Roman Catholics, Platonists and even some Aristotelians. There are two citations in Augustine's works which speak of the priority of reason. In these Augustine was presupposing man's capacity for thought. But there are no passages in Augustine's writings where he puts reason before faith as a method of knowing God.[17] Augustine asserted: "But, if they say that we are not even to believe in Christ, unless they can give a reason that cannot be doubted, then they are not Christians."[18]

Augustine's understanding of the authority of the Bible flowed from his general method, "I believe in order to understand." Scripture was a divine unity for Augustine. No discordancy of any kind was permitted to exist.[19] Augustine had several ways of handling apparent disharmonies. He claimed variously that the manuscript was faulty, that the translation was wrong, or that the reader had not properly understood.[20] When none of these answers seemed appropriate, Augustine sometimes concluded that the Holy Spirit had "permitted" one of the Scripture writers to compose something at variance from what another biblical author had written. For Augustine, these variances were meant to whet our spiritual appetite for understanding.[21]

Variant readings were not an ultimate problem for Augustine because the truth of Scripture resided ultimately in the thought of the biblical writers and not in their individual words. Augustine commented: "In any man's words the thing which we ought narrowly to regard is only the writer's thought which was meant to be expressed, and to which the words ought to be subservient."[22] To keep to the thoughts and intentions of the biblical writers we must, according to Augustine, remember that their purpose was to bring us, not information in general, but the good news of salvation. For Augustine, Scripture was not a textbook of science, or an academic tract, but the Book of life, written in the language of life. When Felix the Manichean claimed that the Holy Spirit had revealed to Manicheus the orbits of the heavenly bodies, Augustine replied that God desired us to become Christians, not astronomers. Such talk, Augustine said,

takes up much of our valuable time and thus distracts our attention from more wholesome matters. Although our authors knew the

truth about the shape of the heavens, the Spirit of God who spoke
by them did not intend to teach men these things, in no way profitable for salvation.[23]

Augustine followed Origen and Chrysostom in accepting the
notion that God accommodated himself to fit our abilities. Augustine spoke about "the Holy Scripture, which suits itself to
babes."[24] Commenting on the Apostle John, Augustine said:

> I venture to say, brethren, that not even John himself has presented
> these things just as they are, but only as best he could, since he
> was a man who spoke of God—inspired, of course, but still a man.
> Because he was inspired he was able to say something; but because
> he who was inspired remained a man, he could not present the full
> reality, but only what a man could say about it.[25]

The Middle Ages

Scholasticism, the work of the School Men, was the medieval
attempt to harmonize faith and reason. John Scotus Erigena
(d. 895) is generally credited with laying the foundation for the
medieval synthesis. He said: "Reason and authority come alike
from the one source of divine wisdom, and cannot contradict
each other. Reason is not to be overruled by authority but the
reverse."[26] This putting of reason over faith began a movement
which culminated in a decisive philosophical shift in the high
Middle Ages. Platonic thought was replaced by Aristotelian reasoning as the basis for theological work.

In the thirteenth century Albertus Magnus determined to make
all of a newly rediscovered body of Aristotelian work available by
making a philosophical and theological commentary on it.
Among Albert's pupils in both Paris and Cologne was a young
Dominican monk named Thomas Aquinas. Partly in response to
the intellectual, political, and military pressure on Europe from
the Arabs, Thomas sought common ground with them by using
Aristotle, whom the Arabs accepted, to create a comprehensive
and systematic philosophical theology.

For Augustine, following Plato, God was known by a divine illumination of the mind, in a very different way from that in which the world was known by the senses. For Thomas, following Aristotle, all knowledge came from the same source—reason based on the data of our sense experience. Thomas declared: "Beginning with sensible things our intellect is led to the point of knowing about God that He exists." [27] Thomas therefore developed five proofs for the existence of God using reason based on our sense experience. The Thomistic arguments were designed to be persuasive to pagans, Arabs, and Christians.

Certain truths, such as the Trinity, exceeded the ability of reason to know them. But reason, according to Thomas, could bring men to the point where such scriptural truths would be accepted on the authority of the church. Theology now moved away from exegesis and became more closely aligned with philosophy.

The medieval synthesis of reason and faith, of Aristotelian philosophy and scriptural teaching, began to break up in the fourteenth century. Reason was separated from faith by the Nominalists, so called because philosophy, they felt, only arbitrarily gave names to things.

Two British Franciscans, John Duns Scotus (d. 1308) and his pupil, William of Occam (d. 1349), turned away from Aristotle to the older Platonic Augustinian thought and criticized Thomism. Science and theology were separate realms. It was impossible to prove theological doctrines rationally. Since Occam had deep reservations about the authority of the corrupt papacy he observed, he proclaimed the revelation of God in the Bible as the authoritative basis for faith. The Scripture was true for Occam, because inspired by the Holy Spirit. [28]

Occam's follower Gabriel Biel (d. 1495) taught Nominalism in Germany at Tübingen. Martin Luther's philosophy professors at Erfurt were Occamists, and his first theology professors were followers of Biel. Luther, in turn, called Occam "beloved master" and "the most eminent and the most brilliant of the Scholastic doctors." [29] Even after Luther turned against nominalist theology, he retained his respect for the anti-scholastic Occamist philosophy.

Luther

Luther was an Augustinian monk at home in the neo-Platonic philosophical milieu of Augustinianism which put faith before reason. Luther said that he learned more from Augustine and the Bible than all other books.[30] His understanding of Scripture followed in that tradition. Luther said:

> For Isaiah vii makes reason subject to faith, when it says: "except ye believe, ye shall not have understanding or reason." It does not say, "Except you have reason ye shall not believe." [31]

For Luther, "in spiritual matters, human reasoning certainly is not in order." [32]

Most important of all was Luther's motivation for turning to Scripture—his personal search for salvation. Luther's question was: How may I find a gracious God? Luther found a God who justified the ungodly in the Bible. The purpose of Scripture was to speak to us of personal salvation. The subject matter of Scripture by which all its parts were rightly interpreted was Christ as Savior. Luther proclaimed:

> The Gospel, then, is nothing but the preaching about Christ, Son of God and of David, true God and man, who by His death and resurrection has overcome all men's sin, and death and hell for us who believe in Him.[33]

For Luther, the inner testimony of the Holy Spirit testified to Christ and thus gave authority to the Word. Luther asked:

> How can we know what is God's Word, and what is right or wrong? . . . You must determine this matter yourself, for your very life depends upon it. Therefore God must speak to your heart.[34]

The imperfect form in which the Bible came to us was an example of the miracle of God's gracious condescension, to clothe his Word in an earthly form. Luther said:

Holy Scripture possesses no external glory, attracts no attention, lacks all beauty and adornment. . . . Yet faith comes from this divine Word, through its inner power without any external loveliness.

Luther concluded:

It is only the internal working of the Holy Spirit that causes us to place our trust in this Word of God, which is without form or comeliness. . . .[35]

Luther's concept of biblical authority followed from his personal relationship to the Bible. For him, Christ alone was without error and was the essential Word of God. Thus, Luther's faith was in the subject matter of Scripture, not its form, which was the object of scholarly investigation. When Luther said of Scripture, "There is no falsehood in it," he was speaking not about technical accuracy, but the ability of the Word to accomplish righteousness in us. See the context of his words:

For we are perfect in Him and free from unrighteousness, because we teach the Word of God in its purity, preach about His mercy, and accept the Word in faith. This does away with unrighteousness which does not harm us. In this doctrine there is no falsehood; here we are pure through and through. This doctrine is genuine, for it is a gift of God.[36]

Calvin

Calvin, like Luther, reacted against the Aristotelian-Thomistic method of the Middle Ages and embraced the older Augustinian tradition. Plato was the best of all the philosophers for Calvin who cited him freely, though not uncritically. Augustine was cited most by Calvin among the Church Fathers. Calvin's basic concepts of the relationship of faith and reason followed the Augustinian "faith leads to understanding" pattern.

For Calvin, all persons had an inborn knowledge of God: "There is within the human mind, and indeed by natural instinct,

an awareness of divinity." [37] Calvin believed that "God himself
has implanted in all men a certain understanding of his divine
majesty." [38] He called it a "conviction" which is "naturally inborn
in all," [39] and "the seed of religion" which was "divinely planted
in all men." [40]

That innate knowledge of God was suppressed by sinful hu-
mans leaving them responsible for their condition. Calvin said:

> Since, therefore, men one and all perceive that there is a God and
> that he is their Maker, they are condemned by their own testimony
> because they have failed to honor him and to consecrate their lives
> to his will.[41]

Because mankind sinfully suppressed this inborn knowledge
of its creator, Calvin noted that God gave "another and better
help" properly to direct us to God the Creator. The purpose of
this revelation of his Word was "to become known unto salvation." [42] The means of this revelation was Scripture which func-
tioned like "spectacles gathering up the otherwise confused
knowledge of God in our minds, having dispersed our dullness,
clearly shows us the true God." [43] It is in this context that Calvin
uttered the oft-quoted statement that "God . . . not merely uses
mute teachers, but also opens his own most hallowed lips." [44]

How can we know the authority of Scripture? Calvin felt that
even to ask such a question was to "mock the Holy Spirit." To
ask the question, "Who can convince us that these writings came
from God?" [45] was like asking "Whence will we learn to distinguish light from darkness, white from black, sweet from bitter?"
The answer for Calvin, as for Augustine, was self-evident: "Indeed, Scripture exhibits fully as clear evidence of its own truth
as white and black things do of their color, or sweet and bitter
things of their taste." [46]

According to Calvin, the persuasion that God is the author of
Scripture was established in us by the internal testimony of the
Holy Spirit. He said: "We ought to seek our conviction in a
higher place than human reasons, judgments, or conjectures, that

is, in the secret testimony of the Spirit." [47] According to Calvin, "human testimonies," which are meant to confirm Scripture's authority "will not be vain if they follow that chief and highest testimony," [48] as secondary aids to our feebleness. Scripture cannot be known as authority outside of faith. Calvin said explicitly: "But those who wish to prove to infidels that Scripture is the Word of God are acting foolishly for only by faith can this be known." [49]

Calvin strove for the Augustinian middle way of the church. He fought against two extremes. He rejected the rationalistic Scholasticism on the one side which demanded proofs prior to faith in Scripture. He rejected with equal firmness the spiritualistic sectarians on the other side who claimed leadings of the Spirit apart from the Scripture. For Calvin, "Word and Spirit belong inseparably together." [50] The children of God, said Calvin, "know no other Spirit than him who dwelt and spoke in the apostles." [51]

Calvin accepted the Augustinian view of the authority of Scripture. The central theme of Scripture was Jesus Christ. The purpose of Scripture was to know Christ savingly. Calvin wrote: "The object of faith is Christ." [52]

God's humbling of himself in Christ was a model of God's method of accommodating himself to us, according to Calvin.

> All thinking about God without Christ is a vast abyss which immediately swallows up all our thoughts. . . . It is evident from this that we cannot believe in God except through Christ, in whom God in a manner makes Himself little, in order to accommodate Himself to our comprehension. [53]

This incarnational style of communication was evident as well in the language of the Bible, according to Calvin:

> For who, even of slight intelligence, does not understand, as nurses commonly do with infants, God is wont in a measure to 'lisp' in speaking to us? Thus such forms of speaking [i.e., the biblical anthropomorphic expressions] do not so much express what God

is like, as accommodate the knowledge of him to our slight capacity. To do this he must descend far beneath his loftiness.[54]

God's method, for Calvin, was "to represent himself to us, not as he is in himself, but as he seems to us." [55]

For Calvin it was not necessary for God to use precise forms of words in Scripture. His saving message was adequately communicated in the varieties of normal human speech.

Calvin noted an inaccuracy in Paul's quotation of Psalm 51:4 in Romans 3:4 and generalized:

> We know that, in quoting Scripture the apostles often used freer language than the original, since they were content if what they quoted applied to their subject, and therefore they were not over-careful in their use of words.[56]

Similarly, Calvin affirmed in his commentary on Hebrews 10:6 that the saving purpose of the biblical message could come through what we would think of as an imperfect form of words:

> They [the apostles] were not overscrupulous in quoting words provided that they did not misuse Scripture for their convenience. We must always look at the purpose for which quotations are made . . . but as far as the words are concerned, as in other things which are not relevant to the present purpose, they allow themselves some indulgence.[57]

Because the purpose of Scripture was to bring us to salvation in Christ, Calvin did not feel that the Bible's teaching had to be harmonized with science. Each was valid in its own sphere. In his commentary on Genesis (1:15, 16), Calvin faced the issue of the relationship of the science of his day and the Bible. The problem was that the moon was spoken of in the Bible as being one of the two great lights with the stars being mentioned only incidentally. Astronomers of Calvin's day had proved that Saturn, because of its great distance from earth, appeared to be less than the moon, but really was a greater light. Calvin wrote:

Moses wrote in popular style things which, without instruction, all ordinary persons, endued with common sense are able to understand; but astronomers investigate with great labour whatever the sagacity of the human mind can comprehend. . . . Nor [is] this science to be condemned. . . . Astronomy is not only pleasant, but also very useful to be known. . . . Nor did Moses truly wish to withdraw us from this pursuit. . . . Had he spoken of things generally unknown, the uneducated might have pleaded in excuse that such subjects were beyond their capacity.[58]

The most recent scholarly biographer of Calvin, T. H. L. Parker, aptly summarized Calvin's views on the authority and interpretation of Scripture: "The creatureliness of the Bible is no hindrance to hearing God's Word but rather the completely necessary condition." [59]

Post-Reformation Scholasticism

Calvin died in 1564. By that time the Roman Catholic Counter-Reformation had consolidated and focused its strength in a rejection of Protestant doctrines at the Council of Trent (1545–1563). In response to Trent, the second generation of Reformers adopted the methods of their adversaries in order to fight them. Post-Reformation Protestants tried to prove the authority of the Bible using the same Aristotelian-Thomistic arguments which Roman Catholics used to prove the authority of the church. Melanchthon, the successor of Luther, and Beza, the successor of Calvin, both endeavored to systematize the work of their masters by casting it into an Aristotelian mold.[60] Thus a significant shift in theological method occurred from the neo-Platonic Augustinianism of Luther and Calvin to the neo-Aristotelian Thomism of their immediate followers. A period of Protestant Scholasticism was thus launched on the European continent in the immediate post-Reformation period.[61]

On the Lutheran side, Melanchthon's work was carried on and crystallized in the *Loci Theologici* of John Gerhard (1582–1637). Gerhard contended that the Scriptures met Aristotle's qualifications for the principles in any science. The doctrine of Scripture, therefore, was not an article of faith, but the *principium* (foundation) of other articles of faith.[62]

On the Reformed side, Beza's Aristotelian rigidifying was furthered in the mid-seventeenth century by the Genevan Francis Turretin (1623–1687) in his *Institutio theologiae elencticae.* Scripture was "the sole principle of theology" for Turretin.[63] While the existence and power of God could be known by reason, redemption and grace could be known in the Word only. Accordingly, the authority of Scripture was the most important subject in theology. Turretin asked a twofold question: "Is the Bible truly credible of itself and divine?" and "How do we know that it is such?" His response was to proclaim that the Bible was inerrant in all matters.

According to Turretin, the Bible is "authentic and divine" because the human writers "were so acted upon and inspired by the Holy Spirit, both as to the things themselves, and as to the words, as to be kept free from all error." [64] He specified: "The prophets did not make mistakes in even the smallest particulars. To say that they did would render doubtful the whole of Scripture." [65] And their inerrant words were inerrantly preserved, according to Turretin: "Nor can we readily believe that God, who dictated and inspired each and every word of these inspired men, would not take care of their entire preservation." [66]

Turretin utilized the Aristotelian-Thomistic method of putting reason before faith to develop his theology.

> Before faith can believe, it must have the divinity of the witness, to whom faith is to be given, clearly established, from certain true marks which are apprehended to it, otherwise it cannot believe.[67]

He applied this method to Scripture as well: "The Bible with its own marks is the argument on account of which I believe." [68] Because reasonable proofs must precede faith, Turretin felt it necessary to harmonize every apparent inconsistency in the biblical text. He refused to admit that the sacred writers could slip in memory or err in the smallest matters.[69]

The method used by Turretin was that developed by Thomas Aquinas. Questions were asked, answers given, objections stated and refuted. The result was a work of systematic precision and great clarity. Turretin quoted 175 authorities in his treatment of the doctrine of Scripture, including most of the Church Fathers, many of his Roman Catholic opponents, and contemporary Reformed orthodox theologians. But, although he claimed to be expounding Reformed theology, he never quoted Calvin.[70]

Many confessional statements had been prepared during the sixteenth century. Turretin felt that yet another was needed, especially to refute weaknesses in the Reformed doctrines of the School of Samur in France. At Turretin's urging, the four Protestant cantons of Zurich, Basel, Bern, and Schaffhausen agreed to the task. J. H. Heidegger of Zurich undertook the writing. The result, published in 1675, was the Helvetic Consensus Formula.[71] Its section on the Bible is directed against textual criticism of the Old Testament. It declared the inspiration of the "Hebrew Original of the Old Testament." This inspiration was found "not only in its consonants, but in its vowels—either the vowel points themselves, or at least the power of the points." The Bible was inspired "not only in its matter, but in its words," the confession stated. In its third article it announced that textual criticism of the Old Testament would "bring the foundation of our faith and its inviolable authority into perilous hazard." [72]

The Westminster Confession of Faith

The English Reformation underwent a separate and distinctive development from that on the continent.[73] There was a Church of England which stood between Roman Catholic and Protestant. Within that church was a Puritan party which pressed for reform in a Calvinistic direction theologically and a Presbyterian direction governmentally. Usually in control and opposed to the Puritans were the Anglo-Catholics who maintained an Aristotelian-Thomistic theology and an hierarchical episcopal form of church government. By the seventeenth century these two church parties were identified with political forces—the Puritans with Parliamentarians and the Anglo-Catholics with the King.

The Westminster Assembly of Divines (1643–1649) was called by the English Parliament to advise them on religious reform. When the English Parliament turned to Scotland for aid in a civil war against King Charles I, Scottish representatives were sent to the English Parliament and to participate in the Assembly.

Eleven persons composed the committee to draft the Westminster Confession of Faith, seven Englishmen and four Scots. The most important outside resources on which the divines drew were the Irish Articles of 1615, prepared by Dublin professor James Usher, and a work of Usher's entitled *A Body of Divinity,* which was a compendium of Reformed theology in use at that time.[74]

Britain was distinctive not only politically, but philosophically. A British anti-Aristotelian Augustinianism was a deep-rooted tradition which was carried on in the Puritan party. The other centrally important philosophical influence was that of Peter Ramus (1515–1572), a Protestant martyr in the St. Bartholomew's Day massacre in Paris. Ramus attacked Aristotelian logic as artificial and contrived and the university curriculum based on Aristotle as confused and disorganized. (Beza would not allow Ramus to teach in Geneva because of his anti-Aristotelianism.) Ramus developed a simplified logic based not on syllogisms, but on self-evident propositions—working in a Platonic way from universals to particulars. From these axioms ideas were laid out in pairs in a neat outline organization. Ramism was introduced in England as a counterforce to the Aristotelian domination at the Royalist-controlled universities.[75] The best known English expositor of Ramist logic was William Temple, whose son Thomas chaired the committee which drafted the Westminster Confession. Thomas Temple's preaching showed that he had mastered the

Ramist logic which was considered just the outlining preparatory to expository preaching.[76]

Philosophically, the Westminster divines remained in the Augustinian tradition of faith leading to understanding. Samuel Rutherford stated the position: "The believer is the most reasonable man in the world, hee who doth all by faith, doth all by the light of sound reason." [77]

Chapter I of the Westminster Confession is entitled "Of the Holy Scripture." The first five of the ten sections of this chapter are an ascending development on the theme of the Holy Spirit's relationship to Scripture. Section i speaks in Platonic-Augustinian fashion of the "light of nature" which is a direct revelation of God in every person's heart. As with Augustine and Calvin, the divines held that man suppressed but could never wholly eradicate that sense of the divine within him. The "works of creation and providence" reinforce in persons that knowledge which has been suppressed and because of which a person is inexcusable for his sin. Thus there is no "natural theology" in the Thomistic fashion, asserting that persons can know God by reason based on sense experience prior to God's revelation. When the Westminster divines spoke of "natural theology," they meant the knowledge which God had implanted in their inner nature. Samuel Rutherford spoke of man's "reasonable soul, which to me is a rare and curious book, on which essentially is written by the immediate finger of God, that natural Theology, that we had in our first creation." [78]

The authority of Scripture in section iv was not made dependent on the testimony of any person or church, but on God, the author of Scripture. There was no recourse, as in Aristotelian Scholasticism, to rationally demonstrable external evidences of the Bible's authority. Edward Reynolds declared that faith is an assent "grounded upon the *authority or authenticalness of a Narrator,* upon whose report . . . we relye without any evidence of the thing it self." [79]

Section v climaxed the development of the first half of the chapter with the statement that, while many arguments for the truth and authority of Holy Scripture can be adduced, only the witness of the Holy Spirit in a person's heart can persuade that person that Scripture is the Word of God. The wording of this section very closely paralleled a work of George Gillespie, one of the Scot commissioners. Gillespie's work was an argument for the union of Word and Spirit against the Antinomians who claimed the Lord speaking to them apart from Scripture. Even in that context Gillespie asserted: "I heartily yeeld that the Spirit of the Lord is a Spirit of Revelation, and it is by the Spirit of God, that we know the things which are freely given us of God." [80]

The last five sections of the Confession dealt especially with how Scripture could be interpreted by a regenerate mind in light of its purpose of bringing us to salvation in Christ. In section vi the saving content of Scripture was clearly delineated: "The whole counsel of God concerning all things necessary for His own glory, man's salvation, faith and life." Scripture was not an encyclopedia of answers to every sort of question for the divines. They asserted that some things are to be ordered by our natural reason and Christian prudence. Those things even included some circumstances of worship and church government.

Scripture was not to be used as a source of information in the sciences to refute what the scholars were discovering. The Westminster divines aligned themselves with the Parliament and supported the idea of a new university in London to teach natural science as the ancient Royalist-dominated universities were not doing. Samuel Rutherford made explicit the fact that Scripture was to mediate salvation, not communicate information on science. He listed areas in which Scripture is *not* our rule, e.g., "not in things of Art and Science, as to speak Latine, to demonstrate conclusions of Astronomie." But it is our rule, he said, "1. in fundamentall's of salvation." [81]

In the final section of their chapter on Scripture, the Westminster divines ended with an affirmation of the union of the Spirit and the Word. They concluded: "The Supreme judge, by which all controversies of religion are to be determined . . . can be no other but the Holy Spirit speaking in the Scripture." Thomas Gataker used the phrase "the Spirit of God in the Word" in speaking of how people might find happiness and contentment. Robert Harris spoke of the Spirit and the Word as one rule: "If you would have your heart made one, you must go all by one rule, inward, the Spirit; outward, the Word." [82]

Despite the pressure from sectarian appeals to private interpretations of the Spirit, the Westminster divines would not give up their firm conviction that it was the Spirit who brought them to the authority of the Word and guided them in interpreting it. Samuel Rutherford, in a tract against the Roman Catholics, asked: "How do we know that Scripture is the Word of God?" If ever there was a place where one might expect a divine to use the Roman Catholic's own style of rational arguments as later Scholastic Protestants did, it was here. Rutherford instead appealed to the Spirit of Christ speaking in Scripture:

> Sheep are docile creatures, Ioh. 10.27. *My sheep heare my voyce, I know them and they follow me* . . . so the instinct of Grace knoweth the voyce of the Beloved amongst many voyces, *Cant.* 2.8. and this discerning power is *in the Subject.*[83]

For Edward Reynolds, the Spirit is the Spirit of Christ who works in the Word to persuade us.

> Which should teach us, what to look for in the *Ministry of the Word,* namely that which will convince us, that which puts an edge upon the Word, and opens the heart and makes it burn, the Spirit *of Christ; for by that only we can be brought unto the righteousness of Christ.*[84]

For the Westminster divines, the final judge in controversies of religion was not just the bare word of Scripture interpreted by human logic, but the Spirit of Christ leading us in Scripture to its central saving witness to him.

The Princeton Theology

The Westminster divines still belonged to the Reformation era in England. Until the middle of the seventeenth century the "Age

of Faith" prevailed. The "Age of Reason" came quickly but un-
expectedly thereafter.

Soon after the Westminster Assembly, John Owen, a younger
contemporary of the Westminster divines, moved English Reformed theology in the same direction as that taken by Francis
Turretin and the continental Scholastics. The threat in both cases
was the rise of biblical criticism. In 1659 Brian Walton published
a Polyglott Bible in England. It introduced variant readings of
the Old Testament text and questioned the antiquity of Hebrew
punctuation. Owen, similarly to Turretin, held that the Hebrew
vowel points were an ancient, sacred, and inspired part of the
Hebrew Bible. Walton was able to hold Owen up to ridicule as
the evidence became clearer that the Hebrew vowel points were
a later addition to the text.[85]

In Scotland, an unofficial and anonymous commentary on the
Westminster Confession appeared in 1650. It manifested a much
more restrictive spirit than the Westminster Confession. It was,
however, often published in the same volume as the Confession,
and many thought it was a product of the Assembly.[86]

British theology moved to the New World in two separate
streams. New England Calvinism was brought and developed by
the Congregationalists, or Independents, as they were known in
England. Scotch-Irish immigration brought another stream of
Calvinism, also modified since the Westminster Assembly. Elements of these two slightly divergent traditions merged to form
the Presbyterian Church in its first American presbytery in 1706.
The significant differences between the traditions have been responsible for splits and reunions which have marked Presbyterian
history since that time.[87]

The Presbyterian Church had no center of theological training
until the founding of Princeton in 1812. Until that time it was
customary for young men to study with pastors as their tutors in
preparation for ordination examination by the presbytery. One
such young man was Archibald Alexander, born in 1772 of
Scotch-Irish parents.[88] In preparation for ordination he studied
Jonathan Edwards, John Owen, John Witherspoon's *Lectures on*

Moral Philosophy, and Francis Turretin's *Loci* in a Latin com-pendium.[89] In 1812, Archibald Alexander was named the first professor of Princeton Seminary and given the task of planning the curriculum. He centered that curriculum in the works of Francis Turretin and the Scottish Common Sense philosophy brought to America by John Witherspoon.

The *Institutio theologiae elencticae* of Francis Turretin was the principal textbook in systematic theology at Princeton Seminary for sixty years until Charles Hodge's *Systematic Theology* replaced it in 1872. Dr. Alexander's biographer reports:

> Dr. Alexander . . . conceived that theology was best taught by a wise union of the text book with the free lecture. Finding no work in English which entirely met his demands he placed in the hands of his pupils the Institutions of Francis Turretin.[90]

Alexander would assign twenty to forty pages of Turretin in Latin and at the next class would ask the students for an exact repetition of what they had read.

Charles Hodge pronounced Turretin's *Institutio* "one of the most perspicuous books ever written." When Hodge replaced Alexander as Professor of Exegetical and Didactic Theology, he continued to use Turretin. Hodge met both the Middler and Senior classes once a week.

> Before the first meeting of either class for the week, the Professor assigned a topic and a corresponding section of Turretin's Institutes of Theology in Latin for previous study. When they met the hour was occupied by a thorough discussion of this subject in the form of question and answer.[91]

Both Alexander and Hodge wrote commentaries on Turretin for classroom use. The influence of Turretin's scholastic theology continued at Princeton until it was reorganized in the 1930s.

The professors at Princeton Seminary vowed to "receive and subscribe" the Westminster Confession of Faith and Catechisms. But the terms used in the Confession's chapter on Scripture were defined by concepts taken from Turretin's *Institutio.*[92] In Hodge's commentary on Turretin in 1833 he wrote that the "authenticity and trustworthiness of the [biblical] narratives" is necessary for a "true faith." [93] Hodge then indicated rational evidences which would demonstrate that authenticity.

The question of errors in the Bible arose in this connection. There is some development within the thought of each of the Princeton theologians on this question. And there is an increasing rigidification from one theologian to another with the passage of years. But, in keeping with their roots in Turretin, when faced with problems, each of them postulated the inerrancy of the Bible in all things. Archibald Alexander wrote:

> And could it be shown that the evangelists had fallen into palpable mistakes in facts of minor importance, it would be impossible to demonstrate that they wrote anything by inspiration.[94]

In his *Systematic Theology,* Hodge declared that the Bible was "free from all error whether of doctrine, fact or precept." [95] Hodge further stated that inspiration was "not confined to moral and religious truths, but extends to the statements of facts, whether scientific, historical, or geographical." [96]

Later Princeton theologians Archibald Alexander Hodge and B. B. Warfield refined the doctrine of inerrancy still further. As their contribution to a series of articles in *The Presbyterian Review* dealing with biblical criticism, they wrote on "Inspiration" in 1881. Hodge, in his part of the article, after admitting the fallibility of human language and judgment, stated:

> Nevertheless the historical faith of the church has always been, that all the affirmations of Scripture of all kinds whether of spiritual doctrine or duty, or of physical or historical fact, or of psychological or philosophical principle, are without any error, when the *ipsissima verba* of the original autographs are ascertained and interpreted in their natural and intended sense.[97]

Thus errorlessness was confined to the original (lost) manuscripts of the Bible. Warfield, in his part of the article, narrowed the burden of proof to one demonstrated error: "A proved error in Scripture contradicts not only our doctrine, but the Scripture claims and, therefore, its inspiration in making those claims." [98] Warfield then added several provisos, one of which was that "no 'error' can be asserted, therefore, which cannot be proved to have been aboriginal in the text." [99] Since the original texts were not available, Warfield seemed to have an unassailable apologetic stance.

Charles Hodge once wrote that "every theology is in one sense a form of philosophy. To understand any theological system, we must understand the philosophy that underlies it and gives it form." [100] That axiom was certainly true of the Princeton theology in its reliance on Scottish Common Sense philosophy.

The founder of Scottish Realism, or Scottish Common Sense philosophy, was Thomas Reid (1710–1796). Developed in an attempt to refute David Hume and Immanuel Kant, this philosophy was brought to America in a fully developed form by John Witherspoon (1722–1794) when he became President of the College of New Jersey (later Princeton College) in 1768. Witherspoon's moral philosophy seems to have been taken over intact by Alexander and Hodge. It influenced generations of students at Princeton Seminary. Between 1830 and 1860 Princeton theologians produced at least fourteen articles endorsing and interpreting the views of Scottish Common Sense philosophers.[101] Archibald Alexander, in a lecture entitled "The Nature and Evidence of Truth," proposed Common Sense philosophy as philosophical "orthodoxy" for succeeding generations of Princeton seminarians.[102]

The principles of Scottish Common Sense philosophy are directly reflected in the principles of biblical interpretation of the Princeton theologians. The first principle of Scottish Realism is that our sense experience is reliable and certain. Witherspoon begins, as all Aristotelians do, with sense experience: "That our senses are to be trusted in the information they give us seems to me to be a first principle because they are the foundation of all our reasonings." [103] What we perceive with our senses really exists. Furthermore, the mind perceives not merely ideas (versus Hume) or appearances (versus Kant) but external objects in themselves.

Influenced by this principle, Hodge showed no trace of the theory of accommodation held by Origen, Chrysostom, Augustine, and Calvin to explain that we do not know God as he is but only his saving mercy adapted to our understanding. For Hodge: "We are certain, therefore, that our ideas of God, founded on the testimony of his Word, correspond to what He really is, and constitute true knowledge." [104]

A second axiom of Scottish Realism was the principle of universality. Thomas Reid held that the first principles of common sense were endorsed by the "universal consent of mankind, not of philosophers only, but of the rude and unlearned and vulgar." [105] Hodge therefore could deal with problem passages in Scripture simply by appealing to "those principles which are in everyman's heart which is fitly called the common sense of mankind." This principle of universality pitted the Princeton theologians against the higher critics who maintained that the ancient world view of biblical times was different from a nineteenth-century view. The critics assumed, as the Princeton theologians did not, that presuppositions and world views varied with historical periods and cultures.

It was natural that a prime antagonist of the Princeton theologians should be Professor Charles Augustus Briggs, whose chief mission in life was to introduce the views of German higher criticism into the Presbyterian Church. Briggs had studied in Germany and joined the faculty of Union Seminary in New York in 1874. He was concerned that "the new conclusions be accepted and interpreted by evangelical Christians and not become a monopoly of the enemies of historic Christianity.[106] The conflict between Briggs and Warfield over the understanding of Scripture in the Westminster Confession is a fascinating and tragic one which has been detailed elsewhere.[107]

Briggs was historically correct in claiming that the *Institutio* of Francis Turretin had become the textbook at Princeton and that "the Westminster Divines were ignored." [108] But the majority of ministers, and through them members, of the Presbyterian Church had been trained for decades to equate Turretin with Westminster and the Reformers. In 1893, the General Assembly of the Presbyterian Church upheld the Hodge-Warfield position on the inerrancy of the original autographs and asserted that this "has always been the belief of the Church." [109] Briggs was suspended from the Presbyterian ministry.

Tensions over the issue of the inerrancy of Scripture increased over the next three decades. Some contended that inerrancy was an "essential and necessary doctrine." [110] Increasing numbers of ministers, however, felt that the doctrine of inerrancy "intended to enhance the authority of the Scriptures in fact impaired their supreme authority for faith and life." [111] In 1927, a special theological commission of the denomination declared that the General Assembly did not have the constitutional power to issue binding definitions of "essential and necessary doctrines." [112]

Thus, the false equation of the theory of inerrancy with the position of the Westminster Confession was never repudiated. Rather, the church simply agreed not to make any interpretation of the Westminster Confession binding.

A Continuing Reformed Tradition

Nineteenth-century theology was not marked only by those who tried to hold onto a scholastic orthodoxy and by those who reacted against it and embraced liberalism. There were others who continued in the Augustinian tradition of the Reformation. In England, for example, there were highly respected evangelicals such as James Orr who did not postulate inerrancy. [113]

Another illustration comes from the Dutch Reformed tradition in the Netherlands in the work of Herman Bavinck (1854–1921) and Abraham Kuyper (1837–1920).

Bavinck and Kuyper both were respected as evangelical and Calvinist theologians by their nineteenth-century counterparts in

America. Both were guest lecturers at Princeton Seminary, and Warfield contributed an enthusiastic introduction to the English translation of Kuyper's *Principles of Sacred Theology*. Their recent successor in the chair of Dogmatics at the Free University of Amsterdam was G. C. Berkouwer, who attempted to bring this tradition into dialogue with ongoing discussions in contemporary theology. This group of Reformed theologians followed the Platonic-Augustinian tradition of beginning in faith and then seeking understanding. Berkouwer declared that it was not theologically appropriate "to discuss Scripture apart from a personal relationship of belief in it." [114] Berkouwer thus reflected Bavinck's attitude that no formal theological method guarantees faith in Scripture. Bavinck wrote: "In the period of dead orthodoxy unbelief in Scripture was in principle just as powerful as in our historico-critical age." [115]

In the nineteenth century, while Hodge and Warfield were rejecting biblical criticism, Kuyper and Bavinck were meeting the issues openly and constructively. Kuyper, for example, wrote:

> If in the four Gospels, words are put in the mouth of Jesus on the same occasion which are dissimilar in form of expression, Jesus naturally cannot have used four forms at the same time, but the Holy Spirit only intended to create an impression for the church which perfectly answers to what went out from Jesus.[116]

Bavinck, like Calvin, recognized a necessary accommodation in the anthropomorphisms of Scripture. He noted: "Even in historical reports there is sometimes distinction between the fact that has taken place and the form in which it is set forth." [117]

This did not detract from the truth of Scripture for Bavinck: "Then finally it appears that Scripture is certainly true in everything, but this truth is absolutely not of the same nature in all its component parts." [118]

The purpose of Scripture was a central concern in this Reformed tradition. Biblical criticism became a problem, according to Bavinck, only when the critics lost sight of the purpose of

Scripture. That purpose, goal, or "destination" of Scripture was "none other than that it should make us wise to salvation." According to Bavinck, Scripture was not meant to give us technically correct scientific information:

> The writers of Holy Scripture probably knew no more than their contemporaries in all these sciences, geology, zoology, physiology, medicine, etc. And it was not necessary either. For Holy Scripture uses the language of daily experience which is always true and remains so. If the Scripture had in place of it used the language of the school and had spoken with scientific exactness, it would have stood in the way of its own authority.[119]

The authority of Scripture is affirmed to us by the internal testimony of the Holy Spirit, according to this Dutch tradition. Kuyper, speaking in a Platonic-Augustinian fashion, said:

> The Reformers wisely appealed on principle to the "witness of the Holy Spirit." By this they understood a testimony that went out directly from the Holy Spirit, as author of the Scripture, to our personal *ego*.[120]

Bavinck became even more specific:

> The real object to which the Holy Spirit gives witness in the hearts of the believers is no other than the *divinitas* of the truth, poured out on us in Christ. Historical, chronological, and geographical data are never in themselves, the object of the witness of the Holy Spirit.[121]

This understanding of the saving purpose of the Bible led Bavinck to deny the post-Reformation emphasis on each word and letter in Scripture.

> In the thought are included the words, and in the words the vowels. But from this it does not follow that the vowel points in our Hebrew manuscripts are from the writers themselves. And it also does not follow that all is full of divine wisdom, that each jot and tittle has

an infinite content. All has its meaning and significance very certainly, but there in the place and in the context in which it comes
forth.[122]

It is in this tradition that Berkouwer confronted the question
of error in Scripture. He first defined "error" in its biblical context. He commented that when error in the sense of incorrectness
is used on the same level as error in the biblical sense of sin and
deception "we are quite far removed from the serious manner in
which error is dealt with in Scripture." In the Bible, what is meant
by error is "not the result of a limited degree of knowledge, but
it is a swerving from the truth and upsetting the faith (2 Tim.
2:18)." [123] Berkouwer acknowledged the "serious motivation" of
advocates of scientific and historical inerrancy, but concluded:
"In the end it will damage reverence for Scripture more than it
will further it." [124]

Berkouwer summarized the developed thought of his tradition:
"It is not that Scripture offers us no information but that the
nature of this information is unique. It is governed by the *purpose*
of God's revelation." [125] The essential fact to remember, according to Berkouwer, was that "the purpose of the God-breathed
Scripture is not at all to provide a scientific *gnosis* in order to
convey and increase human knowledge and wisdom, but to witness of the salvation of God unto faith." [126]

Conclusion

What can this study contribute to current discussions about
the nature of the Bible's authority and how that authority is
known? First, it is historically irresponsible to claim that for two
thousand years Christians have believed that the authority of the
Bible entails a modern concept of inerrancy in scientific and
historical details.[127]

Augustine, Calvin, Rutherford, and Bavinck, for example, all
specifically deny that the Bible should be looked to as an authority in matters of science. To claim them in support of a modern

inerrancy theory is to trivialize their central concern that the Bible is our sole authority on salvation and the living of a Christian life. Christian theologians in the Augustinian tradition have been persons of faith in accepting the authority of Scripture and of devout scholarship in understanding it. The theologians cited above did not claim that the Bible was some kind of direct, unmediated speech of God, like the Koran or Book of Mormon. As Christian scholars, Origen, Chrysostom, Augustine, Calvin, Bavinck all stressed that God accommodated his word to the language and thought forms of limited human beings. We can adequately know God's saving will for us in our imperfect forms of thought and speech.

Second, it is equally irresponsible to claim that the old Princeton theology of Alexander, Hodge, and Warfield is the only legitimate evangelical, or Reformed, theological tradition in America.[128] The old Princeton tradition clearly has its roots in the scholasticism of Turretin and Thomas Aquinas. This tradition is a reactionary one developed to refute attacks on the Bible, especially by the science of biblical criticism. The demand for reasons prior to faith in the authority of the Bible seems wedded to a prior commitment to Aristotelian philosophy.[129] In contrast, Origen, Augustine, Luther, Calvin, the Westminster divines, and Bavinck were decidedly anti-Aristotelian in their theological method. Theologians of the Augustinian tradition accepted the authority of Scripture through the testimony of the Holy Spirit within them. For this Reformation tradition the saving authority of Christ's person known in Scripture authenticates the Bible's authority prior to all human evidences and reasonings.

Third, it is no doubt possible to define the meaning of biblical inerrancy according to the Bible's saving purpose and taking into account the human forms through which God condescended to reveal himself.[130] Inerrancy thus defined could be heartily affirmed by those in the Augustinian tradition. However, the word *inerrancy* has been so identified with the Aristotelian notions of accuracy imposed on it by the old Princeton theology that to redefine it in American culture would be a major task.

Finally, to confuse "error" in the sense of technical accuracy with the biblical notion of error as willful deception diverts us from the serious intent of Scripture. The purpose of the Bible is not to substitute for human science. The purpose of the Bible is to warn against human sin and offer us God's salvation in Christ. Scripture infallibly achieves that purpose. We are called, not to argue Scripture's scientific accuracy, but to accept its saving message. Our faith is not in human proofs but in a Divine Person whose Word persuades us.

THREE VIEWS OF THE BIBLE
IN CONTEMPORARY THEOLOGY

by Clark Pinnock

Clark H. Pinnock is Associate Professor of Systematic Theology at Regent College, Vancouver, British Columbia. In July 1977 he will become Associate Professor of Theology at McMaster Divinity College, Hamilton, Ontario. He has held similar teaching positions at Trinity Evangelical Divinity School (Deerfield, Illinois), New Orleans Baptist Theological Seminary, and the University of Manchester. Dr. Pinnock holds the B.A. in Ancient Near Eastern Studies (University of Toronto, 1960) and the Ph.D. in New Testament (University of Manchester, 1963). He is the author of several books (among them Biblical Revelation: Foundation of Christian Theology *and* Truth on Fire: The Message of Galatians) *and editor of two others,* Toward a Theology for the Future *and* Grace Unlimited. *He is a member of the Society of New Testament Studies, the Tyndale Fellowship for Biblical Research, the Evangelical Theological Society, and the Karl Barth Society of North America; and he is contributing editor to* Sojourners *magazine.*

BIBLICAL INSPIRATION and authority are important issues on the agenda of twentieth-century theology. The church is being compelled to define and redefine her convictions about them. Although it is generally true that the question of authority rises to the surface whenever a human community arranges its beliefs into a coherent system, the prominence of the debate over the Bible cannot be explained in such terms alone. How is it that the question of biblical authority, which lay for centuries almost undebated in the Christian tradition, has suddenly been catapulted into such a dominant position?

It has happened as the result of a *collision* between the traditional belief in the infallibility of the Bible and the critical perspective on the Scriptures, nurtured in the Enlightenment, which saw in it only a record of man's imperfect spiritual and moral evolution. Secular modernity is characterized by a strongly anti-authoritarian attitude, coupled with the determination to study critically the literary sources appealed to in religion. It has removed the Bible from its high pedestal and subjected it to cold scrutiny. The new attitude represents a revolutionary change from the older concepts of inspiration and authority.

The result has been an unsettling *ferment* in which Christians have been forced to ask after the sense in which the Bible is the Word of God. While there are no more than a handful who would not affirm God's Word to be mediated in some sense through it, there is no agreement on the precise nature of biblical authority. What we are witnessing in the debate over the Bible is a series of competing attempts to salvage a viable view out of the wreckage from the collision between traditional doctrine and humanistic criticism.

This chapter surveys the flow of opinion on this important subject in contemporary theology. So that we might be able to position ourselves better in relation to other opinions it examines three influential schools of thought on the subject of biblical inspiration and authority: the liberal perspective, the new reformation stance, and the conservative evangelical standpoint.[1]

Biblical Authority in a Liberal Perspective

Conservative evangelical and even neo-orthodox spokesmen have found it difficult to be fair to liberal theology and its positions. The very term *liberal* in these circles has become almost a whipping boy, a caricature and stereotype of the impressive tradition it actually is. We should not imagine for a moment that we have heard the last of the theological style once advocated by Schleiermacher and Rauschenbusch. It may well prove to have more staying power than its chief detractors, and nothing is gained by misrepresenting what its concerns are. We evangelicals certainly cannot expect a fair and sympathetic hearing until we ourselves give such a hearing to others.

In essence, theological liberalism should be seen as a creative appropriation of and accommodation to the spirit of Enlightenment man. It does not feel compelled to oppose and refute the sensibilities of the modern age, but seeks to relate the biblical symbols creatively to them. It is a theology of experience, but not in any narrow sense. It strives to do justice to the sum total of human experience, including that which is described in the Bible, and wishes to show how the Christian revelation can illuminate the dark places in man's self-understanding. Although in pursuing its ideal of relevance liberal theology has sometimes fallen captive to the intellectual ideas prevalent in the culture, we should not detract from the nobility of its aims.

As a creative synthesis between biblical concepts and modern ideals, a new view of biblical authority was developed in liberal theology. Employing the historical methods developed in the Enlightenment, liberal theology sought to strip the false veneration accorded the Bible in traditional circles and replace it with a proper respect for its human greatness. Though the intention was not to downgrade the Bible, such an impression was given because, before the new view could be heard, the work of demolition first had to take place. Before they could expound upon the positive role Scripture had to play in religion, the liberals felt compelled to destroy every remnant of the older belief in the infallibility of the Bible. In L. Harold DeWolf's textbook in systematic theology, for example, a chapter exposing the fallibility of the Bible *precedes* the chapter on its inspiration so that there can be no misunderstanding.[2]

In its view of biblical authority, liberal theology considers it important to insist that the Bible is a merely human text—written, copied, translated, and interpreted by fallible people. It contains all manner of internal contradictions, moral blemishes, legend and saga, inaccuracies, and the like. It is a collection of intensely human documents and is not an authority beyond criticism or correction.[3] To regard it as God's written Word is an idolatrous perversion of belief which must be dethroned. Although in the past the Bible was regarded as a unique authority in the life of Christians, that day is gone. Its norms no longer bind us. "We are in a new historical situation with a new awareness of our autonomy and responsibility to think things through for ourselves. No longer can we appeal to the unquestioned authority of an inspired book."[4]

It will not do for conservative evangelicals to relegate this negative view of the Bible to a past era of liberal dominance in theology, because it is an ongoing position as fully contemporary as any we are considering. Although perhaps twenty years ago, in the heyday of "biblical theology" and "neo-orthodoxy," respect for the divine authority of the Bible could almost be assumed and taken for granted, no longer is this the case. Once again the Bible is under severe attack, and its supremacy by no means unchallenged. In recent writings, we hear sounded afresh the older liberal note that it is a haphazard collection of documents of mixed value, the authority of which is not qualitatively superior to our own collective opinions. It is theologically diverse, often irrelevant or misleading, and certainly not a final norm of anything.[5] Some are even asking if canonical Scripture is a Christian category, and whether we should limit the locus of the Word to this narrow range of writings.[6]

Yet, despite all that, it would not be fair to judge the liberal view of biblical authority as a basically negative one. To be fair, we would have to add that, questions of biblical fallibility notwithstanding, the Bible is still the indispensable medium through which we apprehend normative divine revelation. Of course the Bible is error-ridden. The divine author was limited to and by the imperfect human writers he had to use in preparing it. Nevertheless, the imperfections all seem inconsequential in comparison with the profound truths to which the Bible bears eloquent witness. We would be remiss in not mentioning this side of the liberal view of the Bible. DeWolf, for example, expresses admiration for the nobility and substance of biblical thought and feeling and sees the providential hand of God guiding in its production. He speaks of its unparalleled influence on mankind and of the importance of studying and obeying it. Of course he does not find divine truth uniformly distributed throughout its extent, and he insists that we read the Bible critically. But, nevertheless, it is a book through which God wishes to address us, and we should be open to his Word.[7]

Liberal theology views biblical authority *selectively*. It is not an infallible authority whose judgments are always binding. There is no authority of that kind. The liberal attitude to Scripture is one of gratitude for whatever guidance the text may afford, together with the freedom to dissent from the canonical spokesmen where they are held not convincing.[8] The respect liberals have for the Bible is not respect for it as an authoritarian book, but as a classical witness of those in whose lives God once worked which can once again serve to alert us to his reality. Ultimately, divine truth is not located in an ancient book but in the ongoing work of the Spirit in the community, as discerned by critical rational judgment.

The weaknesses of the liberal view of biblical authority are quite plain. A preoccupation with the human side of the Bible leads to a serious obscuring of the divine side. Despite the claims the Bible makes for itself, liberals have insisted on reading it as the human record of the human story of man's religious and ethical pilgrimage. Because this was a way of reading the Bible from which the Word of God never came, the Bible fell silent in the liberal churches. What God had to say through the Bible was muffled by an obsession with what man was supposed to have thought up. Liberalism failed to place the critical method itself under the authority of Scripture and as a result lost the sense of the mystery of God speaking in Scripture. William Newton Clarke expressed this sense of loss in a poignant way:

> I tell no secret—though perhaps many a man has wished he could keep it a secret—when I say that to the average minister today the Bible that lies on his pulpit is more or less an unsolved problem. He is loyal to it, and not for his right hand would he degrade it or do it wrong. He longs to speak with authority on the basis of its teaching, and feels he ought to be able to do so. He knows that the people need its message in full power and clearness, and cannot bear to think that it is losing influence with them. Yet he is not entirely free to use it. Criticism has altered the book for his use, and just how far he does not know.[9]

A consequence of the loss of biblical authority was a captivity of liberal theology by the culture and its ruling norms. Liberalism, in the search for relevance, deliberately adjusted the biblical message to the spirit of the times. This was almost inevitable, since it was not the mental categories of Scripture but the experiences of believers which determined the development of theology. Liberalism capitulated to prevailing world-views and came to reflect the intellectual ideas of the age so that the difference between its Christian thinking and the humanism of the culture became harder and harder to detect. It is one thing to translate the biblical faith into understandable categories, but quite another to permit these categories to become the ruling principles for its interpretation.

Biblical Authority According to the New Reformation Theology

Although liberal theologians hoped that the stress on the humanity of the Bible would not result in the loss of the Bible's authority or essential message, what happened was a very considerable sense of loss. A large number of believers experienced a "famine of the Word of God" (cf. Amos 8:11–12). As a result there took place a rebirth of interest in the classical convictions of the Christian creed. Attention again was focused upon the primacy of divine revelation and the finality of the Word of God, not only by traditionally conservative churchmen, but also by a new brand of theology altogether.

New reformation theology, or neo-orthodoxy as it is usually called, is a trend in contemporary theology which attempts to recover the faith of the reformers of the sixteenth century and express it with integrity in the present situation. Reflecting a shift in the culture toward pessimism and a distrust of human wisdom, the new movement emphasized such themes as revelation, salvation, eschatology, sin, transcendence—categories notably suppressed or minimized in liberal theology. However, it would be mistaken to suppose that the new reformation theology was *simply* a return to the older Protestant positions. In fact, it was a synthesis of the old orthodox theology with secular modernity in its new form, comparable with liberalism a few generations earlier. One of the reasons new reformation theology succeeded in causing many liberals to change their position where the conservatives did not was precisely its affinity to liberalism at certain key points. The most obvious example for our purposes is its retention of negative biblical criticism without alteration and without a sense of embarrassment. Another example would be the ambiguity of its talk about the acts of God in history which, while not denied outright as in liberal theology, tend to get relegated in neo-orthodoxy to the realm of faith rather than the public domain. Although God's mighty acts were frequently spoken of, one was usually left wondering whether there was any contact between them and the real world. Moves such as these, which have raised the eyebrows of many critics and prompted questions regarding the meaningfulness of its language, point to the fact that neo-orthodoxy is another attempt to graft onto a basically secular understanding of reality the biblical view of revelation and history. Not surprisingly, tension and a sense of uneasiness have resulted.

A concept of the Word of God is without a doubt the central category in the epistemology of the new reformation theology. The knowledge of God depends entirely on receiving and encountering the Word. For Barth most of all, the Word is mediated in and through the reading of Scripture. Unlike the liberals, Barth does not view the Bible as a record of man's religious ideas, but rather as the definitive witness to divine revelation. In his own life and experience, Barth came to the place where he grasped the divine mystery of the Bible, lost in liberal theology, and recovered the sense of its power to communicate life and truth to the humble reader. To Barth, canonical Scripture is lord and judge of the church, and enjoys priority over all that she does or says. It is in a class by itself.[10]

A comment in his discussion of baptism will shed light on his basic attitude to Scripture: "To oppose tradition is one thing; we think it imperative to do so here. To oppose Holy Scripture is quite another; this we may not do." [11] At the beginning of his treatment of creation, Barth asks why we should take the subject so seriously. The reason he gives is the fact that it is found in the Bible which tells us truth on which we can rely. This is God's witness to himself and to Jesus Christ. As such it is "the infallible Word of God," and the "organ of the Spirit." [12] Granted, Barth is in this respect the most conservative representative of the new reformation theology, but he is also the most important spokesman, and the one whose influence is most likely to endure because of the massive brilliance of his contribution. Conservative evangelicals ought to give Barth a great deal more respect than they have been accustomed to give, and as time goes on I suspect we will increasingly perceive him as the powerful ally he is in the defense of biblical authority.

At the same time there is a certain ambiguity in the manner in which the new reformation relates God's Word to the actual words of the Bible. This emerges from observing the response made to negative biblical criticism, where no effort is made to defend the literal authority of the text from attacks made upon it. Both Bultmann and Brunner belong to this theological family, and they insist on the fallibility of the Bible just as strongly as the liberals do. Bultmann's criticism of the Bible, both in its historical passages and in its doctrinal teachings, is well known, but Brunner too aligns himself with very radical versions of criticism. He too speaks of legendary accretions in both testaments and finds them replete with errors and contradictions. His forthright denial of the miraculous conception of Jesus gave rise to a well-publicized debate with Barth.[13]

Barth also speaks of the imperfection of Scripture and of its capacity for mistakes. It was he who penned this astonishing line:

> To the bold postulate, that if their word is to be the Word of God they must be inerrant in every word, we oppose the even bolder assertion, that according to the scriptural witness about man, which applies to them too, they can be at fault in any word, and have been at fault in every word, and yet according to the same scriptural witness, being justified and sanctified by grace alone, they have still spoken the Word of God in their fallible and erring human word.[14]

The men we hear as witnesses, Barth says, speak as fallible, erring men like ourselves. Their word can be criticized in its historical and ethical content, and even in its religious and theological teachings. There are parts of the Bible we can make no use of, and lacunae, inconsistencies, and overemphases abound in it. And yet, Barth warns us against pronouncing in any specific case that its biblical writer has erred. "From what standpoint can we make any such pronouncement?" [15] We must not misrepresent Barth. Although he insists on allowing perfect freedom for critical investigation, he actually speaks only of a capacity for errors, not of errors themselves. Indeed he denies anyone the right to act as judge of Scripture. While preaching the errancy of the Bible, Barth practices its inerrancy. His reader would have to look long and hard into the *Church Dogmatics* before he could come up with any charge of error in the intended teachings of the Bible. Barth pointedly affirms that the most insignificant of the biblical witnesses possesses an incomparable advantage over his most scholarly successors. Our proper place is beneath the Word, not above it. [16] Nevertheless even Barth still creates an ambiguity in the relationship between the Word and the biblical words which is hard to contain.

We can identify two basic motifs operating behind the new reformation position. One is the great importance placed on the freedom of God. We should not suppose that God's Word is "frozen" in the words of the Bible. [17] God has free disposal of the verbal character of Scripture—to use it or not use it, to use it in the way he pleases. In that case, we must think of the "Word" of God as a dynamic, somewhat elusive entity paradoxically related to the biblical text, but also floating free of it. Barth even says: *"Theopneustia* [inspiration] is the act of revelation in which the prophets and apostles in their humanity became what they were, and in which alone in their humanity they can become to us what they are." [18] We must think of the Word then, not as a fixed, inscripturated quantity, encompassed by these writings, but as an event which takes place in a suprascriptural activity of the Spirit in the heart of the believer. The testimony of the biblical witnesses is not a deposit, but operates as an event in which the Word remains free. [19] To identify the Word with Scripture would in Barth's judgment violate the free sovereignty of God which means that man must have no control over his work or word. By stressing God's freedom in this way Barth loosens up the moorings of theology in Scripture, for others if not for himself.[20]

A second motif to note in the new reformation view, which distinguishes it from both the liberal and conservative alternatives, is the emphasis it places upon revelation as a personal encounter with God. Bultmann puts it plainly:

> What, then, has been revealed? Nothing at all, so far as the question about revelation asks for doctrines—doctrines, say, that no man could have discovered for himself—or for mysteries that become known once and for all as soon as they are communicated.[21]

Revelation is instead existential truth, truth which transforms man's life, and not objective propositional truth at all. Emphasis distinctly shifts away from viewing the Bible as a collection of inspired propositions, and turns rather toward seeing it as the unique medium of a living encounter with God. While not entirely denying that revelation has a verbal component, the new reformation view stresses the point that revelation is fundamentally a matter of nonverbal living experience. Emil Brunner has distinguished between "it-truth" and "thou-truth," and locates revelation in the existential realm. John Baillie also underlines this point strongly by contrasting the knowledge *about* God—revelation as information—and the knowledge *of* God himself. In revelation we are given, not truth concerning God, but the living God himself.[22] This kind of language occurs repeatedly in writings of the new reformation school. The authority of the Bible is vested, not in the doubtfully infallible language of the text, but in the powerful will of God to let it become a "Word" for us in the moment of decision. To anyone troubled by difficulties in the Bible, this view seems immediately attractive because of the way it locates the truth of Scripture, not at the level of correctness and accuracy, but on the higher plane of God's faithful dealings with us. In that case the Scripture could not be said to err on account of the erroneous judgments it is thought to make, inasmuch as its truth is of an existential kind. Critical theories which touch only the words of the text cannot damage the Word of God conveyed through them. A harmony of biblical authority and critical honesty seems to have been achieved.

By way of evaluation, the new reformation view of the Bible is an attempt to preserve the older reformational confidence in its divine authority without having to reject what it sees as advances made in critical Bible study under the auspices of Protestant liberalism. In addition, neo-orthodoxy was troubled by the apparent absence of spiritual power in orthodoxy, and therefore sought to reach behind it to the earlier Reformers. In doing so, it was assumed that this view of Scripture, as well as its use, was different. Conservative evangelicals would be ungrateful not to appreciate the seriousness of this effort to affirm responsibly the mystery of God speaking in Scripture. But there are difficulties with the view also. Chief among them is the ambiguity postulated in the relation of the Word to Scripture. In a desire to prevent man from gaining control over God's Word, the new reformation position creates a bifurcation between the two by espousing a dynamic concept of revelation which tends to locate the Word, not any longer in the Bible, but in man's experience of faith. Of course the view is worded in terms of an act of God's self-disclosure, not of religious self-consciousness, but the end result is not very different. The irony must be obvious. Was it not the great liberal Schleiermacher who grounded theology in the religious self-consciousness, and was it not Barth who thundered against the humanizing of revelation? The answer is positive, but our conclusion is that in this regard neo-orthodoxy is closer to liberalism than it admits. Its celebrated break with the liberal perspective was not as complete as is claimed. Not much is gained by putting the Word at the center if the "Word" turns out to be an elusive and mystically present "something" behind and beyond the words of a book which is admitted to be full of errors and contradictions. What is to prevent such a "Word" from being mauled and manipulated by the preconceptions of the readers? The new reformation view of biblical authority will not do, because it is a half-measure which falls short of the biblical claim that God's Word is present unambiguously and directly in the words of Scripture, a text which can judge and correct our wayward minds, and shed light upon them.

Biblical Authority in Conservative Evangelical Theology

The curious coalition known as conservative evangelicalism is held together, howbeit tenuously, by its doctrine of Scripture, as much as anything else. Its constituents, who come from a myriad of denominational traditions, are drawn together by the need they feel to counter the negative view of the Bible they see in liberal theology and the positive, but ambiguous view they find in new reformation thinking. Essential to evangelical spirituality and theology is the attitude to Scripture which regards it as the Word of God written. Although it can be fairly argued that this attitude is more closely similar to the ancient convictions in the church about inspiration than are either the liberal or the neo-orthodox views, still it would not be accurate simply to equate them. The situation we face in defending the Bible today against negative criticism is very different from the challenges to which Calvin and Augustine had to respond, and the arguments that have been devised are different also. The reason the Princeton theology has become so influential in conservative evangelicalism is precisely because its position on inspiration was worked out in this new situation, in a way relevant to it. The argument of hoary antiquity has some force, but it cannot relieve us of the necessity to show how the conservative evangelical doctrine of Scripture can stand in the light of current biblical scholarship. We will have to get down to work and explain how our position on inspiration is a more scriptural, coherent, and consistent alternative than the other options.

Although Protestant orthodoxy confesses both the divine and the human element in the Bible, as it also does in Christology, it has been happier affirming its divine authority than admitting its human characteristics. This is perfectly understandable, given the polemical situation in which liberalism could see little else than the limitations and frailties of the Bible, though the position will remain imbalanced until full justice is done to the human traits as well. Conservative evangelicals have been able to argue with good success that the notion of God speaking and giving man his Word is very central in the Bible, and that Scripture is nothing other than an extension of this modality of revelation. Although modern discussions tend to overlook it, the Bible itself places a good deal of emphasis upon God committing his Word to speech and to writing.[23] Writings in this perspective seldom miss the opportunity to adduce testimony from the lips of Jesus, the apostles, and the prophets in which the claim is made to have received and to be delivering the very Word of God in human speech. Warfield set the example for this line of argument, and others have added to it.[24] The conclusion is drawn that the biblical teachers set forth a concept of plenary, verbal inspiration, and the appeal is made to recognize the vital connection between acknowleding their authority, especially the authority of Jesus, and the attitude to the Bible we adopt.[25]

The Bible for conservative evangelicals is revelation in writing. Though manifesting human traits, it is the source of heavenly instruction. Therefore, we read it with an ear open to what God wants to teach us. The Word is not a mystical "something," but the meaning of the words themselves. Certainly the Bible mediates an encounter with God, but equally it is a communication from God about subjects he wishes us to believe and apply. It is a book of divine wisdom, not merely human opinion, and we should go on listening to it even when it offends and challenges us.

Veneration for the divine authority of Scripture in opposition to the liberal view has made it difficult for conservative evangelicals to do justice to the human side of Scripture. This has led in turn to difficult public relations with other positions who insist on it and also to painful internal dissensions over what is often interpreted as a concession to liberalism. In a pendulum reaction against modernism, conservative evangelicals find it difficult to accept the evidence that God in his written Word has stooped to our infirmity and given us a Bible with human limitations. A false piety has grown up which would seek to protect the Bible from its own humanity, fearful lest a close examination of its inconsistencies, duplicate passages, seemingly pointless details, would detract from its divine authority. In his recent book, the dean of evangelical theologians, G. C. Berkouwer, has come out against this perverse resistance to having God's Word truly enter the human realm and be subject to the conditions of other writings. He makes his point, not out of any desire to have colleagues who are more up to date critically, but because he thinks it essential that we gratefully receive God's Word *as he gave it* and in no other way. We do not probe God's mind by ignoring the actual nature of the Bible, but by studying it, and taking into account the cultural context, and the human qualities. Berkouwer's concern is the same we had for the new reformation position. We do not find the infallible Word of God in abstraction from the biblical words, but right there in them. Conservative evangelicals must submit to the Bible honestly and not try to soften the contours of the text. If we do that, we are doing the same thing that we criticize liberals for doing—not facing up to the Word in its full objectivity.[26]

An excessive veneration and overbelief about the Bible has been a problem for some conservative evangelicals. The very desire to identify God's Word with the words of the Bible sometimes produces an almost superstitious regard for every detail of it. There have even been Christians who have postulated the inspiration of the Septuagint, and Vulgate and King James translations, and even the infallibility of the vowel points in the Hebrew manuscripts of the Old Testament. In a day when the divine authority of Scripture is being questioned, the atmosphere can become charged and the slightest uncertainty be interpreted as a sign of declension. It is therefore felt necessary to plug all the gaps in the argument, and present an impregnable flank. There is an acrimonious dispute at the present time in conservative evangelicalism related to this, a debate over the degree of perfection or errorlessness of the biblical text, and it promises to have a very divisive effect on the movement unless it can be defused.

On the one hand there stands a group of scholars upholding the position of B. B. Warfield, who defended the total trustworthiness and perfect infallibility of the Bible, and who considered it a matter of great importance that no error be admitted as belonging to the Scriptures.[27] Scripture, God's Word, could no more err than God could lie. Biblical inerrancy is implied in biblical inspiration. Against that position there stands a second group who could, if they wished, name James Orr or now G. C. Berkouwer as their spokeman; they are dissatisfied with Warfield's case for biblical inerrancy and what it implies for biblical exegesis.[28] From their ranks have been appearing a number of important queries about inerrancy which should not be ignored. Referring to some of them and attempting to weigh them might help us get beyond the present impasse. As a defender of biblical inerrancy, I believe we need to listen to these qustions and concerns, and assess their significance.[29]

Question One: Is inerrancy scriptural? In every defense of biblical inerrancy it is maintained that the notion is scriptural, that is, a concept taught by Jesus and the apostles. They all received the written Word in an attitude of total trust, and recognized no errors of any kind in it. On closer examination, however, the issue is not quite so straightforward. As soon as one examines the manner in which inerrancy is understood in relation to the Bible by its proponents, it becomes clear how subtle an idea it is; we are forced to ask whether it is really scriptural or simply an inference drawn by godly minds. For example, inerrancy is taken to refer to the autographs, not the present copies of Scripture, whereas it is likely that Jesus and Paul in teaching about inspiration had reference to the imperfect copies in their possession. If they did, one cannot press the point that they taught inerrancy in this sense. Further, most defenders of inerrancy, following Warfield,[30] understand inerrancy relative to the intention of the text, not absolutely of its every detail. In this view, there are errors in the Bible, but they do not overthrow inerrancy because they do not belong to the intended, but only the unintended teachings of the Bible. When we consider the *subtlety* of the inerrancy inference, we must be cautious in claiming without qualification that the Bible teaches exactly that. It is a possible inference, but not the only one.[31] And, if it is an inference we choose to draw, as I do, we should be scrupulously careful in defining exactly what we mean by it, and claim no more certainty for it than we should.

Question Two: Is inerrancy a logical corollary of inspiration? Rivalling the argument from Scripture in weight is the often-registered point that if the Bible is God-breathed it must logically be free from every error; how could it be anything other than inerrantly flawless? Although this position may seem reasonable at first sight, it is difficult to see how human beings would be capable of drawing such inferences from the fact of inspiration. God uses fallible spokesmen all the time to deliver his word, and it does not follow that the Bible *must* be otherwise. We are simply not in a position by sheer logic to judge how God ought to have given his Word. The logic of the case for inerrancy has been confused by a mistaken piety and the errorlessness of the Bible defended, not so much out of the conviction that it *is* inerrant as from the belief that it *must* be.

Question Three: Is inerrancy meaningful? A term is meaningful when it conveys the sense intended without too many qualifications being required. Some evangelicals have trouble with inerrancy on these grounds. It is not that they disagree with the thought behind the word. The word itself has become a liability because of the misunderstandings it creates. Inerrancy, as applied by many of its scholarly exponents, is actually hedged about by numerous exceptions. A purported "error" has a number of hurdles to jump before it can qualify as an error. It must belong to the nonexistent autographs, something that cannot really be proved. It must be proved beyond doubt, again a practical impossibility. Further, it must belong to the intended assertions of

Scripture. Inerrancy is a somewhat untestable and unfalsifiable assertion. We could say that because the writers of Samuel did not intend to give us a chronologically perfect account of the history of Israel, the errors in Samuel do not invalidate biblical inerrancy. But what is gained talking in this way? Why speak of inerrancy if errors are fairly easily accommodated to it? A writer like Harold Lindsell will claim to defend strict inerrancy, but not actually do so.[32] He is not denying errors in the text of the Bible *without qualification* since he admits there are errors of a casual kind, as in grammar or numerical exactness, and errors of other kinds in the copies of Scripture modern readers have always had to use. Even as strict and passionate a book as Lindsell's evidences that unsuitability of the ferm *inerrancy* for what he contends. It should at least be understandable to those who side with him, whether they agree or not, why there are evangelicals who prefer not to speak of biblical inerrancy and feel it is misleading to do so. Until we are sensitive to this preference, as a godly concern for meaningful speech, the present unjust situation will continue in which a party employing the slogan *inerrancy* will be considered more orthodox than those reluctant to use it, even though there is no substantial difference between their actual views of the text! Let us battle for the Bible, but not for a slogan.

Question Four: Is inerrancy an epistemological necessity? Defenders of inerrancy sometimes play on the fears of Bible readers. If the Bible is mistaken on a single point, how can we believe it at all? Religious certainty would be destroyed if a flaw were to exist in Scripture. When we consider the fact that no Bible in existence is flawless, logically we should stop trusting the Bible at once. Fortunately, the appeal must not be taken very seriously, since believers in inerrancy go on reading and believing their imperfect copies and live with the very uncertainty the argument says they should not have. But the fact that the argument would be made at all and be so widely accepted is troublesome. To say that unless every point can be established, the entire edifice will come crashing down seems to indicate the fortress mentality of an orthodoxy in decline. When the awareness of God speaking powerfully through Scripture begins to subside, it is necessary to cling to rationalistic arguments in order to defend the Bible, and scholastic orthodoxy is born. It is certainly difficult to understand why God, if he deemed errorlessness epistemologically so crucial, did not take greater care to preserve the text errorless, and how it is that the errant Bibles Christians have always had to use have been so effective for millennia. Obviously the argument based on epistemology is itself very doubtful.

In another twist to the argument, it is sometimes claimed that belief in biblical inerrancy is the only sure bulwark against apostasy.[33] If biblical inspiration had been identified instead of inerrancy, the argument would have had more plausibility. But as it stands, it is far from true. What right have we to argue that a view of inspiration cannot be high and strong unless inerrancy is implied in it? It is a gross overstatement which can only have bad effects itself; indeed, it may well be a self-fulfilling prophecy. Imagine a student, convinced that a single flaw in Scripture invalidates the whole Bible, confronting what he sincerely believes to be a surd inconsistency in the text. Is he not likely to abandon all his convictions forthwith, and would he not be less likely to do so had he not been persuaded to equate inspiration and inerrancy? Perhaps this is a "domino" effect we should fear more than we do, namely, the polarizing of conservative evangelicalism to the extent that any seriously questioning person will be compelled either to embrace a new liberalism or muffle his inquiries.

The epistemological argument should be turned around in yet another way. Is it not suicidal, as Orr claimed long ago,[34] to make the authority of the Bible stand or fall upon such a question as whether the disciples were meant to carry a staff or not, or whether rabbits chew the cud or not? We recall the quip: "Weak is the faith that hangs upon a hare!" The evangelical view of inspiration is not strengthened in people's eyes by getting boxed into such absurdity. Such arguments discredit our position: one error in a tiny detail of Scripture invalidates its inspiration and opens the floodgates to a host of Bible-denying theories leading inevitably to liberalism. Rather than bolstering up the position, such logic only weakens our cause and closes doors to our testimony.

Question Five: Is inerrancy theologically decisive? As a result of the polemics surrounding this issue, inerrancy has been so exalted as to become a chief characteristic of Scripture for many. Instead of placing emphasis upon the saving truth of the Bible to bear witness to Christ, attention is focused rather on the precise accuracy of minor details. This unfortunate development does not do justice to the kind of book the Bible is. Minute inerrancy may be a central issue for the telephone book but not for psalms, proverbs, apocalyptic, and parables. Inerrancy just does not focus attention correctly where the Bible is concerned.

Further, it is alarming to consider how similar to the spirit and method of the Pharisees this preoccupation with the minutiae of the Bible is. While fretting over details, they were closed to the actual message of the Bible as Jesus announced it. Their "high view" of biblical inerrancy served to conceal their unbelief. Though it is said Jesus held to the Jewish view of Scripture in his day, surely that is not so. He did not teach us to concern ourselves chiefly with niceties of detail, but to hear God's Word issue forth afresh from the text. Neo-orthodoxy disliked Protestant orthodoxy precisely because it concentrated on rationalistic arguments and did not display joyful confidence in the self-evident authority of Scripture, preached in the power of the Spirit. Not much will be gained by making a case for inerrancy if what is needed is the kind of Spirit-directed exegesis of the text in which God is once again heard to speak with power and authority through it.

Question Six: Is inerrancy critically honest? One of the most serious difficulties the theory of errorlessness faces is the Bible itself. To defend it in a way that does not evade the phenomena of the text requires incredible dexterity and ingenuity. It is not so hard if, like Warfield, we do not take the difficulties very seriously.[35] But it is not easy at all if we do.[36] The tragedy in conservative evangelicalism today is the fact that the defense of inerrancy is often carried on by those still wrestling with a list of difficulties that has not changed for a hundred years, while the evangelical biblical scholars who work very closely with the text tend not to publish their opinions about inerrancy. The result is twofold: the defense of inerrancy often presents artificial harmonizations on stock questions,[37] while no one is giving us much help with handling the newer issues such as "canonical shape," redaction criticism, the history of transmission within the Bible, and so forth. Obviously the evangelical fixation on errorlessness has prevented us from getting ahead in biblical interpretation, and explains why we must turn to non-evangelicals to get help working out the details.[38]

Question Seven: Ought inerrancy to be the test of evangelical authenticity? Lindsell says that no one who rejects biblical inerrancy has any right to claim the "evangelical badge." [39] If the reader has followed the questions up until now, he will have to conclude that at least some grounds for hesitation about inerrancy exist which do not stem from unbelief but from honest questioning. In that case, we must judge it unjust and extreme to identify evangelicalism with the Warfieldian theory of perfect errorlessness. Where will such a view lead? To the excommunication of dissenters from recognized "evangelical" institutions and denominations? No doubt it will have to, and indeed already has. We should stop this process before it goes any further. As one who defends biblical inerrancy, I urge charity toward those whose hesitation over inerrancy is due to their honest judgment and not to any weakness of their evangelical convictions. Inerrancy must not become a "shibboleth" to be wielded like a sledge hammer to destroy the work of God.

In order to be fair to the inerrancy position, however, something must now be said in its behalf. Although some have no doubt defended it unwisely, prompting such questions as these, it is nevertheless a strong, excellent term when properly used. In speaking of the Bible as "without error in all that it affirms," the Lausanne Covenant sets a good example for us. It does not just thrust a slogan forward without qualification, but places the principle in a relation to biblical interpretation. When this is done, and when the Bible is reasonably defended, few of the queries about inerrancy refer to it or damage it. I am convinced that most of the conflict over inerrancy could be avoided if the defenders of it, on the one hand, would explain carefully what they mean and do not mean by it, and those who are hesitant, on the other hand, would make it plain that their hesitation has nothing to do with a decline in their respect for Scripture. Unless we do so, we will not find ourselves taken very seriously outside our own ranks or have our critique of the liberal and neo-orthodox positions listened to. Worst of all, we will experience acrimonious division and strife where there ought to be fraternity and cooperation.

Having issued a warning against excesses on the inerrancy side of this debate, it is only right and proper to express an *equal* concern about the dangers on the moderate side. If there are some weaknesses in the case for inerrancy as usually presented, there are also flaws and potential dangers implicit in any case for biblical errancy. What is there to prevent these evangelicals from handling the Bible like liberals do—assigning some texts into limbo, and canonizing the texts now held to be suitable and acceptable? Although Dewey Beegle exposed numerous flaws in the case for biblical inerrancy, he does himself operate with an important distinction between primary and secondary revelation in Scripture, and he believes it necessary to determine which "word of the Lord" in the text may be the "most authentic." He feels that when biblical writers, like Paul, for example, move away from their basic insights and begin to delineate the details, they may prove to be less reliable.[40] In a recent, well-publicized book, *Man as Male and Female,* Paul K. Jewett put such a view into practice in the case of Paul's teaching regarding women. Seeing in Paul's epistles some evidence of male chauvinist views, Jewett concludes that Paul, being heir to both Rabbinic and Christian traditions, occasionally betrayed a sub-Christian viewpoint, and should not be followed where this happens. Jewett evidently rejects exegetical possibilities that these difficult texts can be harmonized with the clearcut feminism of Galatians 3:28. As a result, one is forced to conclude that in Scripture God does not always speak, requiring the reader to determine where he speaks and where he does not. In principle this seems to be liberal, not firmly evangelical, theological methodology, and therefore a disturbing doctrinal development. It is more troubling because it issues from a theologian of such stature, erudition, and obviously orthodox convictions in general. Though our respect for him remains high, we cannot fail to register deep misgivings, and the feeling that, if this is tied to the case against Warfieldian inerrancy, then it reveals deeper flaws in itself than any exposed in the questions above.[41]

The fact of the matter is that both the inerrancy position and its opponents within conservative evangelicalism need to do further work on their concepts of inspiration. The way beyond our present impasse is not to strike out against those questioning inerrancy, or to fall into the trap of supposing that, once rid of Warfield's obsessions, we sail on a quiet sea, free of perils. It is not so! The evangelical movement could easily divide into two camps over this question: a defensive fundamentalism armed with a slogan and a neo-liberalism stumbling ahead into more and more biblical denial. This need not happen. But happen it will unless God's Spirit leads us to listen to his voice expressed in the whole company of believers and away from the militancy and fear that often surround our discussion. It also means we ought to write theology communally, so that God can check our individual folly by means of fellow believers.[42]

Conclusion

As a result of the rise of negative criticism, the authority of the Bible has been seriously impaired for many people. Although the erosion has not been equal in all groups (e.g., black Christians in North America have not been greatly affected) and is far more prevalent in academia than in the churches, nevertheless there is a crisis which should not be ignored. James D. Smart, who is not a conservative evangelical himself, feels that the Bible is in a very bad way in the churches and that the situation is the most potentially dangerous of any crisis we face today.[43] The intimate connection between the Bible and the community is such that the church which forgets the Bible is in danger of forgetting its own identity and mission.

Although the issue of inspiration and authority was forced upon us by recent intellectual history, it may be that in the providence of God there will emerge out of it truly significant theological reflection about the subject. Surely God, and not only negative critics, is calling us to a deeper appreciation for and understanding of his written Word. Warfield made a great contribution, but his is not the last word. It was the inception of a long process of theological reflection that has not finished yet. If it took centuries to hammer out the trinitarian and Christological definitions, why should we suppose it will take less time to produce an adequate theology of revelation itself? May God grant us a team of godly, evangelical thinkers who will give themselves wholeheartedly to this task and who will view their work not as the definitive statement, but as building blocks in a great cathedral to whose building they will have contributed, even though most of them will be forgotten.

The prime theological issue which became evident in our survey of options on biblical authority is the need to maintain with equal force both the humanity and the divinity of the word of Scripture. Failure to do that is at the heart of the dissatisfaction we feel with all the positions mentioned, including our own. It seems to be a natural tendency for us to view the divine and the human elements in Scripture as competitive and exclusive of one another. Instead of seeing them in congruence, we tend to suppress or minimize one in favor of the other, especially in the present heated polemical situation. In view of the fact that conceptualizing any circumstances where both God and man are present and active, such as in the Bible or in Jesus himself, is the most difficult theological task possible, it is no wonder many false starts and bad moves have been made. Many tiny oak scrubs must spring up before the great oak tree takes a deep hold on the earth. The way ahead on this subject is undoubtedly to avoid at all costs the pendulum effect of stressing the humanity or the divinity of the Bible exclusively, and to get on with a balanced appreciation for both. There is no need for us to solve the mystery of how the Bible can be the Word of God in the words of man. But there is a great need for us to recognize that it is.

Jesus once told the story of two sons. One of them said he would not work in his father's vineyard but in the end did so, and the other son said he would go to work, but did not. Jesus was emphasizing the importance of actually doing the will of God, and not just claiming to. As James later wrote, we are to be doers of the Word, and not hearers only (1:22). In the case of biblical authority, we need to recognize that what God desires from us is not empty praise for the book but obedience to it. Yet it often seems that we conservative evangelicals are more concerned to prove the Chronicler was accurate, than to stand by what Amos or Jeremiah said. How ironic it would be if the very stalwarts on behalf of biblical authority were the ones who fell into the trap of allowing North American materialism and worldliness to be the norm for our behavior rather than the Word we so highly praise. The great peril of conservative religion in our day, as it was in Jesus' time, is that it will be used to bolster up unbiblical behavior behind a cloak of impeccable orthodoxy. If so, we are nothing more than liberals ourselves, who neglect and suppress the Word and go willingly into cultural captivity. God did not give us his Word simply to reinforce our earlier ideas and structures, but to critically challenge and renew them. Perhaps this ought to be the test henceforth of evangelical soundness.

What will keep us sound in the faith will not be our strenuous rationalistic efforts to make the case for the Bible air-tight. It is the Spirit of God in mighty power moving through the church who keeps us whole and maintains the balance. In an era of true reformation and revival, there is not an obsession with the inerrancy of biblical details because there is an overwhelming sense of the power and authority of God speaking through the Word by the Spirit. The moving of the Spirit accomplishes more on behalf of biblical authority than all the arguments of conservative evangelicals ever could. Without this work of renewal, I fear, we are shut up to the alternatives of a threatened defensive evangelicalism opposed by an equally intellectualistic neo-liberal rationalism, both of which from their distant extremes threaten to damage the quality of truth. But with the moving of the Spirit we can expect to experience a deep delight in and gratitude to God for his Word. Let us pray for a new generation of theologians who know the power and authority of the Scriptures and who can minister to the renewed multitudes in whose lives God is so evidently working today.

THE BIBLE'S OWN APPROACH
TO AUTHORITY

by Berkeley Mickelsen

Berkeley Mickelsen is Professor of New Testament Interpretation at Bethel Theological Seminary in St. Paul, Minnesota, a position he has held since 1965. Prior to that time, he was a professor at Wheaton College and the Wheaton Graduate School over a period of twenty years. He is author of Interpreting the Bible *(Eerdmans, 1963) and was a contributor to* Can We Trust Our Bible? *He is also author of the article "Romans" in the* Wycliffe Bible Commentary *and "Hebrews" in the* Holman Study Bible. *Dr. Mickelsen holds the B.A. from Wheaton College, the B.D. and M.A. from Wheaton Graduate School, and the Ph.D. in New Testament and Early Christian Literature from the Division of Humanities of the University of Chicago.*

THE QUESTION OF authority is crucial in our times. Questions of war, race, oppressed minorities, rights of women, rights of the unborn, religious pluralism—all of these questions and many others demand answers with authoritative bases.

Assumed and Actual Authorities for Modern Man

How do we determine where authority lies? Although in recent years we have lost confidence in the institutions—political, educational, ecclesiastical—that formed the authorities for most people, some still give their highest allegiance to the democratic processes or societal norms, while some rely on coherent rational ideas. Others insist that the church, despite its failures, is still the authority to guide people in their complicated life situations. In practice, peer groups often seem to set the norm and thereby become the authority.

In spite of all these possibilities, separately or in combination, one has a haunting suspicion that simplistic shortcuts are often taken: an action or idea is right because the person says it is, or perhaps because two or three agree on it. We are reminded of the refrain in the Book of Judges: "Every man did what was right in his own eyes" (Judg. 17:6; 21:25; cf. Deut. 12:8). Saying that something is right when the basis for judgment lies only in an

77

individual or individuals does not constitute true authority. True authority lies *outside* of ourselves, although we must respond to make that *outside* authority our own.

Questions about the Authority of the Bible

During the last of the nineteenth century and throughout the twentieth century, the nature of the authority of the Bible has been intensely debated. Much of this debate has paralleled studies about how books of the Bible were written, the role of authors and editors.

Every scrap of evidence, every clue that would illuminate the human side of the Bible was carefully pursued. The time-honored axiom "Because God is its author, the Bible is authoritative" came to be counterbalanced by some scholars with another axiom, "Because men are its authors, the Bible is not *intrinsically authoritative*": it has only an *illuminating, relational authority* in the sense that the Bible influences and helps our understanding of ourselves, our world, and of God.[1] Sometimes study of the human side of the Bible was accompanied by a dedicated naturalism. Supernaturalism was ruled out automatically. Anything miraculous in the Bible, naturalistic scholars explained by ordinary causes. Many other scholars, however, who investigated the human side of the Bible without such biases, saw that when God so chose, there were miracles and powerful revelations. These scholars also saw how often God chose to act with people in their own ordinary ways and thought patterns. The combination of these two kinds of action by God gives the Bible authenticity. But it does not attempt to change the Bible into a modern book with current ways and thought patterns to describe life in this earthly scene.

Since the Bible includes such a wide variety of literary forms and so diversified a content, it is quite possible to select certain passages and declare that God is the author. But by changing the selection, one can also say: "Man is the author." Ecclesiastes, Esther, and parts of Job certainly give us human opinion and deeply felt human convictions. But that is only part of the Bible, and we need to consider the whole picture. It seems more accurate to say that the Bible is *co-authored* with God in control. God energized and worked with many human agents, some named and some unnamed.

The Authority of the Bible Is Not Imposed

No individual scholar or group of scholars should try to construct an abstract definition of an authoritative book as the first step in their case. While they could then declare that the Bible meets their definition and is thereby authoritative, with careful scrutiny another group could probably say: "The Bible does not really meet your own definition; therefore, it is not authoritative." Or they could say: "Your definition is inadequate, so even if the Bible did meet your definition, this would not make it authoritative." This kind of imposed authority only leaves the Christian caught between the battle of the "experts."

Protestants have sometimes been caricatured as holding the absolute authority of the Bible on doctrinal questions without regard to the need for interpretive procedures. One writer who seems to reflect this approach is C. Duraisngh:

> The claim of absolute and sole authority [of the Bible] in doctrinal matters in Protestant Churches is a dubious and dangerous one. It is dubious because . . . the ultimate authority for Protestants is not and never has been *Scripture alone,* but Scripture as interpreted in the tradition of their denomination or school of thought. . . . It is also dubious, for it is a claim to have a "direct" access to the Bible, ignoring two thousand and more years of history of interpretation. . . . A concept of the Bible apart from the tradition that limited it through a canon is a myth and therefore to claim any absolute and objective authority for the Bible is dubious.[2]

Duraisngh fails to realize that evangelical Protestants have read their Bibles carefully for centuries and that they have been aware of countless biblical passages with specific doctrinal teachings and differences of opinion as to how some of these passages should be interpreted. Their conviction that the Bible alone is the authority in doctrinal matters ruled out many human speculations that claimed authority but contradicted biblical truths God had made known to his people in many different situations. Of course, these basic truths had to be gathered and evaluated hermeneutically. Since the Bible is a collection of "case histories," the hermeneutical evaluation had to be done carefully, with a humble dependence on the Spirit, and wherever possible in fellowship with groups of faithful Christians. But usually the result was a direction, a course of action, a statement of faith that made the truth of God vital for some need of their day. When the interpreter makes wise use of authoritative materials, the process is never mechanical. The Bible is our sole authority to tell us about the Absolute and his will for mankind.

Obviously, doctrinal statements that have been formulated throughout the history of the church to meet the needs of a particular occasion or threatening heresy cannot be final. Life is a changing scene, and new variables make reformulation necessary. Regardless of how informed or misinformed we are by the vast array of data in contemporary human knowledge and research, *the authority* to which we go is still God and his Word, the Bible. We must restate or reformulate, not because we want to water down truth or weaken lifestyles or conduct, but rather because we want to strengthen statements of truth, lifestyles, and conduct.

Key Terms Associated with the Authority of the Bible

Several key expressions are persistently used in discussing the authority of the Bible. These need to be firmly understood if we are to grasp how much is involved in authority and how many people participated in the production and recognition of the Scriptures.

Authoritative materials (oral and written) before the canon. The materials in the Bible were authoritative *before* they became an official part of the canon. For example, the *prophets* proclaimed their messages orally with an authoritative "Thus saith the Lord." The separate *proverbs* passed orally from person to person for centuries before they became part of the Old Testament canon. The *poetry* (outside the prophets) in the psalms and elsewhere, expressing joy, sorrow, frustration, also circulated orally. *Laws* and *statutes* were known in Abraham's time (Gen. 26:5), showing that Moses was not the first to disseminate laws. However, laws, prophetic oracles, proverbs, and poetry eventually came also into written forms, and, as in oral forms, were recognized as authoritative.

The same is true of the New Testament. The sayings and deeds of Jesus, recounted orally at first, later were also written down. Our gospels are the final written form. Letters of the apostles, usually sent to specific churches, eventually reached a larger audience who also regarded them as authoritative. So before there was an Old or New Testament, there were authoritative materials.

What does canon involve? Canon involves two separate processes on the part of God's people, the first for the Old Testament and the other for the New Testament. By 100 B.C. or earlier, the materials now found in the Old Testament were recognized to be authoritative. By a similar process, between A.D. 100 and 350, Christian churches recognized the materials now found in the New Testament to be authoritative. No council decision determined the canon; the councils only recognized what had already been accepted in practice as authoritative. A number of factors were determinative in this process: (1) material was used frequently in public reading; (2) the ascribed author or the important figures in the book had to have positive stature with the people of God; (3) materials showed prophetic or theological coloring to history (for example, Judges and Acts); (4) writings revealed connections with the life of the people (Wisdom literature) and with the foreboding pressures that seemed destined to sweep the people away (Apocalyptic); (5) writings showed freshness and historical proximity to distinctive acts of God.

This is not a complete list of the factors involved, but it is sufficient to show that this process resulted in a collection of materials that the people of God in every generation have accepted as "authoritative." During the 250 years when the New Testament canon was being formed, more gospels were being circulated than those of Matthew, Mark, Luke, and John; we still have some of them. Most readers who examine these apocryphal gospels agree that they have some value, but they also agree with the verdict of the early Christians that these gospels are not in the same category as the great four. The same is true of the rest of the New Testament. Other epistles, acts, and apocalypses were circulating, but they did not become part of the canon. The process established and eliminated books that circulated. The New Testament canon of twenty-seven books has now stood for over 1625 years.

This is an oversimplified treatment of the process of canon. The full picture is hard to get because we do not have an abundance of data or evidence. But there is abundant evidence on the *outcome* of canon. The writings of the Bible were considered to be in a distinctive category. Other writings were recognized as useful and helpful. But the materials in the canon were different; they had been tested through a long process. Succeeding generations were of no mind to void the results of many years of sifting.

Revelation. The Hebrew and Greek words behind this term mean "to reveal," "disclose," "uncover." In Greek, half of the occurrences of the noun (*apokalupsis*) and one-third of the occurrences of the verb (*apokaluptō*) refer to the revealing or disclosing of truth(s). In Deuteronomy 29:29 (Heb. 29:28) there is a contrast between "hidden things" and "the things that are revealed."

> The secret things belong to the Lord our God; but *the things that are revealed* belong to us and to our children forever, *that we may do all the words of this law.*

The things revealed are found in the words of the law. Note the importance of the concluding clause. Revealed things are not just *preserved* in words; they are revealed to be *observed* and *carried out*.

Revelation involves truths about God, men, the world, life, death, destiny. It focuses upon a right relationship with God that touches every phase of our lives. Legalism makes the commandments to be supreme. Law makes the personal being of God to be supreme. Revelation puts us into a dynamic relationship with the Revealer. In revelation our authority is the disclosed will of One whom we love because he first loved us (1 John 4:19–21). Authority does not consist in confrontation with Infinite Force. Rather authority is acknowledged in voluntary surrender to concerned Being.[3]

Inspiration. In the classical text about inspiration—2 Timothy 3:14–17—the Old Testament (Timothy knew it as the Septuagint) is called "holy writings" (v. 15). These writings were to "instruct," "teach," "make wise" Paul's disciple Timothy. He was to respond by faith in a vital relationship with Jesus Christ. The outcome of the power of these writings and of Timothy's response is salvation. Every Scripture passage of the Old Testament is *energized by God* and *beneficial* to change the man of God.

The prophet Micah indicted the rulers of Israel. He condemned the false prophets for leading the people astray by crying "Peace." He said that political rulers, prophets, and priests seemed to be interested only in money (Mic. 3). To the false prophets who claimed that the Lord was in their midst and no evil could happen to them Micah pronounced: "Jerusalem shall become a heap of ruins" (3:12). Drawing a sharp contrast, Micah told what made him different from his contemporary false prophets, priests and leaders.

> But as for me, I am filled with power
> with the Spirit of the Lord,
> and with justice and might,
> to declare to Jacob his transgression
> and to Israel his sin (Mic. 3:8).

Micah was energized by God. The Spirit of the Lord was with

him. He did not speculate about *how* God energized him or *how* the Spirit of God filled him. Like Paul in his writing to Timothy, Micah was concerned with the purpose of this filling: *to declare to Jacob his transgression and to Israel his sin* (3:8b). Micah's contemporaries did not accept his authority or respond to the authoritative message that he proclaimed. But Micah knew God and today we can read Micah's words and affirm: "This man speaks with prophetic authority."

What is inspiration? It is the energizing power of God in the lives, discourse, and writings of his servants so that from these writings men can see life with God as supreme. They can know that they ought to move, live, and have their being in relationship to God.

Inerrancy. The converse of the statement "The Bible teaches truth" is that the Bible does not teach error. Strangely enough, this simple statement "The Bible does not teach error" has caused controversy because it ignores *how* the Bible teaches truth. It also says nothing about what standards one uses to judge error. Harold Lindsell characterizes inerrancy in this way:

> This Word is free from all error in its original autographs. . . . It is wholly trustworthy in matters of history and doctrine. . . . The authors of Scripture, under the guidance of the Holy Spirit, were preserved from making factual, historical, scientific, or other error.[4]

Two main areas seem to be implicit in Lindsell's statement. The proposition "without error" seems to declare: (1) the Bible avoids all incorrectness in any particular assertions; (2) the Bible avoids deception, deceit, any kind of falsehood.[5]

In the first of these two areas—correctness or incorrectness in particular assertions—the standard one uses to judge error (incorrectness) is crucial. There are a variety of possibilities. We may apply the standards adhered to in biblical times or our modern standards, or a mixture of the two; and we may vary the degree in which we use them, from applying them rigorously, or less rigorously, but still carefully, down to applying them only carelessly.

Let us take a well-known example of how Matthew locates an Old Testament reference. After Judas' betrayal of Jesus, Judas received no comfort from the chief priests (see Matt. 27:3–10). In his despair he hung himself. Since he had returned the thirty pieces of silver, the chief priests were puzzled as to what they should do with the money. It was "blood money" because Jesus had already been condemned. So the money could not be put into the temple treasury. With the money they purchased the potter's field as a burial place for strangers (Matt. 27:7). From that day until the time when Matthew wrote, this field was called "the Field of Blood" (Matt. 27:8).

Matthew concludes the incident with an Old Testament quotation:

> Then was fulfilled that which was spoken through the prophet Jeremiah saying: "And they took the thirty pieces of silver [Zech. 11:13b], the price of him upon whom a price had been established whom they priced from the sons of Israel [Zech. 11:13a], and they gave them [Zech. 11:13b] for the field [Jer. 32:6–9] of the potter [Zech. 11:13a,b], just as the Lord commanded me" [Exod. 9:12, Septuagint] (Matt. 27:9–10).

Where Matthew has "they took" and "they gave," Zechariah has "I took" and "I cast." Now if we view Matthew's quotation the way we normally quote Scripture in our day, we would expect to find the passage quoted verbatim from Jeremiah. But when we examine the passage carefully, we see that almost all of the passage comes from Zechariah. Furthermore, the phrases from Zechariah have been rearranged. We find only three words that come from Jeremiah: "for the field" (Jer. 32:7,8,9). The concluding phrase "as the Lord commanded me" or something similar appears in several places in the Greek Old Testament (for example in Exod. 9:12), but it is not part of the quotations in Zechariah or Jeremiah. Matthew apparently used it to show that both Zechariah and Jeremiah were under God's orders.

If we judge the way Matthew locates this quotation by modern standards, we should insist that Matthew begin: "Then was fulfilled that which was spoken through the prophets Zechariah and Jeremiah. . . ." We should expect Matthew to end his quotation with the word "adapted" to show that he made some changes. Of course, Matthew has not done this. So those who judge Matthew by our modern standards will conclude: "This is the wrong way to make a quotation."

If we judge Matthew by standards of his own time, we will see why he wrote as he did. In Matthew 27:7–8 the word "field" occurs three times. The chief priests purchased the field with Judas's money—the thirty pieces of silver. In the original Old Testament passage Zechariah is talking about the value which the people put upon himself and the Lord. Using typology, Matthew applies this to Jesus. Zechariah said nothing about the purchase of a field. But Jeremiah does (see Jer. 32:6–9,10–15,25,43–44). For Jeremiah the purchase showed God's concern for his people. Jeremiah said that after the exile God would bless his people in their land. Using typology, Matthew connects the field purchase of Jeremiah with the thirty pieces of silver and the potter spoken of by Zechariah. So the three words "for the field" are the reason for Matthew's formula: "through the prophet Jeremiah, saying" (27:9). If we judge Matthew by the standards of his own time, this is an acceptable way of doing it. He wanted to stress the field so he located the passage where the field was mentioned. He saw no need to speak of adaptation because a fresh application demanded adaptation.

It is no wonder that discussion about inerrancy has caused such tension. The careful student faces hundreds of examples like this one above (various kinds of details). Unless he stipulates what standards he is using and how rigorously he is applying these standards, the issue is hopelessly confused. Sometimes shortcuts are attempted. Some proponents of inerrancy have responded in situations like this: "Matthew does not *intend to teach* anything about the source of the quotation. He only *intends to teach* that Jesus' death fulfilled certain things that the Old Testament pictured by way of anticipation." This is a form of rationalization. Matthew certainly intends to use the Old Testament the way he is accustomed to using it.

The inerrancy discussions of modern times (involving all of these ambiguous factors) do not contribute to a high view of inspiration or to a strong case for the authority of Scripture. Instead of discussing what the Bible does *not* do (i.e. "have any errors") we need to concentrate on the positive note. *The Bible teaches truth.* It teaches truth in the ways and manners of expressing *truth in ancient times.* Because God energized his servants, the truths taught in many different ways are superbly effective. Let us thank God for the Scriptures just the way they are. Their ancient form and style are among the great proofs of their authenticity.

Illumination. Illumination involves the bringing of insight and understanding to believers who have been and are being changed. Where we have an authoritative message, we need illumination to perceive the profoundness of that message.

We have just defined inspiration and illumination as they are involved with the authority of the Bible. We have affirmed (in the discussion on inerrancy) that the Bible teaches truth. But how does one find an adequate definition of the authority of the Bible? God did not instruct John to add an extra chapter to the Book of Revelation in which he listed sixty-six books, told why each of them was authoritative, and concluded by telling why the sum total was authoritative. There is no such formal definition of the authority of the Bible.

But there is much in both the Old and New Testaments concerning authority. Genuine authority, i.e., who and what are authoritative and how men should respond to all aspects of authority, is one of the most profound and widespread themes of the Bible.

With no formal definition of biblical authority given us, we must examine the Scriptures to see exactly what is involved. There we will see that (1) biblical authority is directly connected with *the initiative* and *endeavors of God* with selected *leaders* of *his* people (Israel in the Old Testament and Abraham's seed or the true Israel in the New Testament); (2) biblical authority is associated with *God's disclosures of his deep concern for the people themselves* (Israel; the church); (3) biblical authority is seen in *God's powerful deeds and disclosures in Christ;* (4)

biblical authority involves *God's mighty efforts through the Spirit with the apostles, prophets, and fellow workers* who proclaimed a unique gospel (Gal. 1:11–12) that transforms those who respond.

Biblical authority rises out of a unique series of relationships: God's relations with selected leaders of Israel; God's relations with the people of Israel; God's actions in Christ; God's relations with the leaders of the church; God's relations with his people who comprise the church. God is not a mere military conqueror whose authority is established by the mechanical exercise of his infinite power. His power will bring about the universal totality of his Reign. But the supremacy of God's authority is seen in the nature of his concern or pathos. Because of who he is, he addresses man. In whatever way man responds to God, man establishes God's authority. Total harmony is the final outcome of God's authority.

The Nature of Authority in the Old and New Testaments

Both Old and New Testaments contain many words or expressions that designate authority or show a response to that authority. Authority is personal. God is personal. God's representatives are persons chosen by him. Those who respond to God or who fail to respond are persons. Authority is felt and perceived in dialogue, by in-depth person-to-person communication. Its nature becomes clear with man's awareness of the true structure of the universe, of where he stands in creation, and why God stands as supreme.

The Authority of God

Christians have one God, not three. The concept of three "persons" of the Trinity is a means of adhering to the New Testament revelation about God while the New Testament also agrees with the Old Testament that the Covenant God of Israel is one unique Being. All our thought categories are stretched by God's disclosure about himself in Christ. The term *God* here may mean God the Father; it may mean God the maker of the Covenant; it may mean God the creator of heaven and earth.

Authority, power, right to exercise rule. Just prior to the ascension of Jesus, the disciples asked him if he was going to restore the kingdom to Israel at this time (Acts 1:6). His answer was: "Not yours is it to know [understand] the times and the seasons which the Father has placed under his own authority" (Acts 1:7). Jesus said that they would receive power for their mission after the Holy Spirit came upon them. God the Father "knows" totally, completely, at one grasp, all that is involved in the times and seasons. God's knowledge of destiny is his alone. This knowledge does not belong to man. God has placed such knowledge under his own authority or power. God has authority or power to conceal and not to conceal. God has told us enough of his plan so that we know he has a good and great plan. We know that God is in control. But the details and all the decisive turns of human history we do not know. God's authority underscores both his hiddenness and his revealedness.

God's authority or power includes not only the plan of history, much of which has not been revealed, but also the regulating of the eternal destiny of all persons who come on the scene of history. The disciples, Jesus declared, must not fear those who can take away only their physical lives. Rather they are to fear the One who constantly has authority not only to end physical life but also to cast persons into Gehenna, the final place of punishment (Luke 12:5). What makes God's authority so awesome is the unending character of human existence. How we live on earth shows our true loyalty. Where we will live after death shows God's true authority.

Glory, majesty, power and authority belong to God. The Book of Jude states that these qualities belonged to God before time began; they belong to him in the present; and they will be his for all the ages, i.e., forevermore (Jude 25). Authority belongs to God because of who he is. God had authority before he created. Following creation God shows his love, his holiness, his compassion, and his wrath toward those who presevere in their sins. In all these responses, God's authority—his inherent right to direct others—becomes clear.

King, Kingdom, Judge. When the biblical speakers and writers referred to God as a King, as the One who has a Kingdom, as One who is and will be Judge, they knew they were using figurative language. Kings and judges exercised tremendous control over the lives of people. The territory or district over which the king ruled or where the judge carried out his duties was often small by our standards. But kings and judges had full authority in their spheres of control. This is the point of correspondence that makes the metaphor effective—the authority over the lives of others possessed by one living in a certain geographical sphere is transferred to God, who has no such human limitations.

Psalm 47 celebrates the covenant God of Israel, the Lord, the One who is the Most High as "a great King over all the earth" (v. 2). The psalmist asks the people to "sing praises to our King" (v. 6). He then returns to the earlier theme: they are to sing praises *because* God is the King of all the earth (v. 7). The psalm ends (vv. 8–9) with a picture of all peoples being gathered along with Israel.

The New Testament further emphasizes God as king. He is a sovereign, a king, and a lord in 1 Timothy 6:15–16. He is the King of the ages (or King of the nations, which fits the context better) in Revelation 15:3.

Other passages in the Old Testament speak of God as a judge. Abraham knows that the Judge of all the earth will do right (Gen. 18:25). Hannah celebrates the knowledge that the Lord will judge the ends of the earth (1 Sam. 2:10).

In the New Testament Paul speaks of a day in which God will judge the world in righteousness by a man (Christ, the one raised from the dead) whom he (God) has appointed (Acts 17:31).

These expressions stress the universality of the Lord's authority. They show that this authority will also bring complete harmony in the universe. God is not a static, unmoving authority. The King and Judge of the Bible will act to end an old epoch, and, by a carefully worked-out transition, will introduce a whole new epoch of splendor, beauty, peace, and meaningful existence.

Lord, Master, Sovereign of the Covenant. The third and fourth chapters of Exodus recount the incident of the burning bush and Moses' ensuing dialogue with the Lord. When God told Moses that he would lead Israel out of Egypt, Moses protested against taking the role of leader. He objected that the phrase "God of your fathers has sent me to you" was insufficient authority. The people would ask for the name of this God of their fathers; what should Moses reply to them (Exod. 3:13)? God answered Moses: "I am he who I am" [6] (Exod. 3:14). The "I am" announces the one who just "is."

This one who just "is" was the Lord, "the God of your fathers, the God of Abraham, the God of Isaac, and the God of Jacob."

In Isaiah 45:5 we read: "I am the Lord, and there is no other, besides me there is no God." The prophet continued: "That men may know, from the rising of the sun and from the west, that there is none besides me; I am the Lord, and there is no other" (Isa. 45:6). *The authority of the Lord is in this very uniqueness of Being.* He has the authority of One who is, of One who acts, of One who cares, and of One who commands.

Micah took up the latter theme. He asked: "With what shall I come before the Lord . . . ?" He mentioned cultic customs of Israel and of non-Israelites: calves for burnt offerings, thousands of rams, ten thousands of rivers of oil, even child sacrifices. He concluded by telling what the Lord has really commanded: "to do justice, and to love kindness [steadfast love], and to walk humbly with your God" (Mic. 6:6–8). The Lord, Sovereign of the Covenant, discloses his Authority. He asks man to do what the Lord does, to love what the Lord loves, and humbly to walk with God, i.e., have fellowship with God. Though the Authority is in a unique Being distinct from man, man can be so attuned to God that there is a oneness of thought and purpose. This kind of Authority is not a threat but an enthralling motivator to life on the highest plane.

Exalted Position. Many psalms describe God as in the height (of heaven), as the Most High, (e.g., 47, 92, 93). In Psalm 7 the psalmist asks the Lord to vindicate his just cause: "Let the congregation of peoples assemble around Thee, and over it [the congregation], return to the height [of heaven]. The Lord is judging peoples; judge me, O Lord, according to my uprightness, according to my integrity upon me (Ps. 7:7–8, Heb. vv. 8–9). The height stresses God's authority and right to judge. The psalmist closes on a note of thanks for the Lord's righteousness: "I will praise in song the name of the Lord, most High" (Ps. 7:17, Heb. v. 18).

Besides "God" there are three names for God in Psalm 91:1–2. "One who dwells in the shelter of *the Most High,* who lodges himself in the shadow of *the Almighty*—a person in this kind of fellowship—will say to *the Lord:* 'My refuge and my fortress, my God in whom I trust.'" The lofty position that designated authority was no barrier to fellowship. The Hebrews who knew God as their authority were not disturbed by the paradox: the Most High was so close that they could dwell with him.

Need for Priestly Intercessors. In the latter part of Exodus a refrain is often repeated: "They [Aaron and his sons] are *to serve me* as priests" (cf. Exod. 28:1,3,4,41; 29:1; 30:30; 40:13,15). God spelled out the office of these intermediaries: "I will consecrate the tent of meeting and the altar; Aaron also and his sons I will consecrate, *to serve me* as priests" (Exod. 29:44). In the Old Testament, priests were those who served God and stood between him and his people.

Their task is clearly stated in another refrain: "And *the priest shall make atonement for him* for the sin which he has committed, and *he shall be forgiven*" (Lev. 4:35, cf. 4:20,26,31; 5:6,10,13,16,18). The sin offerings were for priests, rulers, the whole congregation, and for any member of the common people. When any person or group committed a sin unwittingly, i.e., not willfully, the individual brought a goat or a lamb. Specified acts of the sinner and of the priest were part of the restoration. The priest made atonement and the individual sinner was forgiven. Atonement and forgiveness ultimately belong to God as the authority. In the priesthood we see those through whom God worked.

Commands: the Lawgiver; God's concern for people and their response. God's authority comes through clearly in his commands. James does not want Christians to be judging one another (James 4:11–12). Christians who judge each other speak evil of the law of loving one's neighbor as himself. There is only one Lawgiver and Judge, namely God. James wants to know who is so bold as to be trying to take God's place. Because God is the Lawgiver, his commands must be kept distinct from men's commands.

Love for God is more than an emotional experience. "Now the love for God is this that we are keeping or observing his commandments" (1 John 5:3). John adds: "And his commandments are not burdensome" (1 John 5:3). Love plus obedience brings harmony without any foreboding sense of duty. The highest view of authority in the Bible is obedience surrounded by love.

Covenantal basis for God's relationship to his people. After Peter healed the lame man at the gate of the temple, the gate called Beautiful (Acts 3:1–10), Peter spoke to an astounded group of people. He preached the good news about the resurrected Jesus, repentance, and the blotting out of sins (3:19–20,26). He said that Jesus the Messiah was the prophet whom Moses spoke about in (Deut. 18:15; Acts 3:22). Peter reminded his readers of their privileged position: (1) they were sons of the prophets, i.e., they were descendants and disciples of the great line of prophets in Israel; (2) they were *sons of the covenant,* i.e., they were under obligation to follow the covenant (Acts 3:25).

God continued his promises and laid down a new covenant in Jeremiah (Jer. 31:31–34; cf. Heb. 8:7–13; 10:15–18; 13:20; Luke 22:20; 1 Cor. 11:25). Thus God showed his authority in revealing the terms of the first and also the second covenant (see Heb. 10:5–10: the will of God in terms of animal sacrifices and the will of God in terms of the offering of the body of Jesus Christ, once for all). A covenant occurs when in a special way God makes known his will, and when biblical writers take note that this special occurrence is a covenant. The second covenant was an everlasting covenant (Heb. 13:20), so God's authority was behind this arrangement forever. Sin will be banished under this covenant and unending harmony established. God's authority is grounded in his covenants and the way he works out his plan. Because the plan is great and the covenants do not tell all of the details, the authoritative plan of God involves much more than what we now know about his new covenant. But God's authority is clear if we take seriously his promises and his covenants together with what he has done thus far to put these promises and covenants into action.

Communication of truth. The biblical writers simply said, "God spoke." Consequently, we have no right to give our own private interpretation of prophecy found in Scripture (2 Pet. 1:20). True prophets as they *spoke* did not bring on or produce their prophecies by their own will. Rather these prophets *spoke* from God while or because they were being moved or put in motion by the Holy Spirit. So when the prophets *spoke,* God *spoke* (2 Pet. 1:21). God *spoke* to the fathers in or by the prophets (Heb. 1:1). In the last of these days—New Testament times—God *spoke* in a Son (Heb. 1:2). In the Letter to the Hebrews, the writer saw God as still *speaking* (Heb. 12:25–28). He warned about the consequences for any who turned away from this One who was *speaking* from heaven. What and how God speaks shows his authority. His voice that once shook the earth at Sinai will shake not only the earth but also the heaven. God communicates both by what he says and what he does. God's words and deeds show his distinct authority.

The biblical writers were also aware of "holy writings," or "holy scriptures." Paul used this language when he referred to "the gospel" as being promised beforehand "through God's prophets in the holy scriptures" (Rom. 1:1–2). Paul meant the Old Testament. In New Testament times the Old Testament consisted of a collection of scrolls. For example, there was probably one scroll for Isaiah and one scroll for the so-called minor prophets. There was no book form as we now know it. A scroll long enough for the whole of the Old Testament would have been unworkable. Its sheer size would have made it impossible to handle. Hand-printed letters were large, so even though there was no division of the letters into words (just solid lines of letters), manuscripts were long. This was true of both Hebrew and Greek. The adjective "holy" (*hagios* in Rom. 1:2) does not mean that these writings were untouchable; it simply means they were dedicated or consecrated to communicating truth that God wanted his people to have. The quality of the writings comes from the character of the Communicator, whose presence loomed large in the lives and experiences of his people.

Timothy's mother was a Jewess and his father was a Greek. He was well known in Asia Minor in the towns of Lystra and Iconium (Acts 16:1–3). He had become a Christian out of a Jewish background (2 Tim. 1:5). Jewish people in Asia Minor would have read their Old Testaments in Greek (see how often Paul quotes the Septuagint or some other Greek translation). Timothy's heritage was a real bonus for him. From childhood Paul said, "You have known the holy writings (hiera grammata)" (2 Tim. 3:15). Because of God's authority these "holy writings" were able to make Timothy wise for salvation when he responded by faith. Every scripture passage in these writings was energized by God and was useful (profitable, beneficial) (1) for instruction; (2) for reproof; (3) for restoration; and (4) for training in the realm of uprightness (2 Tim. 3:16). The purpose of these four things is that God's man (generic) might be *proficient* in his service for God and permanently equipped for every good deed. Holy or dedicated writings are to bring about holy or dedicated people. The God who energized the writings also empowered his people who responded (Phil. 4:13; 2 Tim. 2:1; Eph. 6:10; Col. 1:11). This he continues to do. Thus God's authority is seen in the close connection between his communication and his action.

The Authority of Christ

Christ's authority can be seen in much the same areas as those that showed the nature of God's authority. In most of these categories there is an abundance of materials. A few examples will serve to sketch out the broad picture.

Universality of Christ's power or authority. When four friends of a paralytic brought him to Jesus, they even went to the pains of removing part of a roof to let the man down on his cot before Jesus (Matt. 9:1–8, Mark 2:1–12, Luke 5:17–26). Jesus' first words to the man were: "Child, your sins are forgiven" (Mark 2:5). The scribes and Pharisees were stunned by this, insisting that Jesus was blaspheming, because God alone could forgive sins (Luke 5:21).

Jesus' answer stressed his power and authority. It was just as easy for him to forgive sins as to restore the man's health (Matt. 9:5, Mark 2:9, Luke 5:23). Jesus then commanded the paralytic to rise up, take his cot, and go home, "that you might know that the Son of Man has *authority upon the earth* to forgive sins" (Matt. 9:6, Mark 2:10, Luke 5:24).

Just before giving the great commission to evangelize the nations, Jesus talked about himself: "All power or authority *in heaven* and *upon earth* has been given to me" (Matt. 28:18). That includes all that exists in both the earthly-material realm or the eternal-heavenly realm. Jesus claimed and demonstrated supreme authority in both spheres.

Royal and judicial authority. Nathaniel was astonished that Jesus saw him under the fig tree even before Philip invited Nathaniel to meet Jesus (John 1:48). Nathaniel exclaimed: "You are the son of God, you are king of Israel" (John 1:49). The full significance of Jesus' kingship would not then be clear to Nathaniel. Later Jesus told Pilate that at that time his kingship was not of this world (John 18:36). "If my kingdom were of this world (contrary to fact condition in the present time) [which it is not], my servants would be fighting."

In the Book of Revelation, in connection with the seventh trumpet, there is the announcement: "The kingdom of the world becomes the kingdom of our Lord and his Messiah and he will reign forever and forever" (Rev. 11:15). Christ is "King of kings and Lord of lords" (Rev. 19:16; cf. 17:14).

In Ephesians it is very clear that some will be excluded from the future kingdom. Sexually immoral or covetous persons (both sins being forms of idolatry) have no inheritance in the kingdom of Christ or of God (Eph. 5:5). The kingdom which lies ahead is also a present reality: from the domain of darkness we have been transferred "into the kingdom of the Son of God's love" (Col. 1:13). Christ's reign or kingdom points to his authority both in the present and in the future.

Christ is also the supreme judge. The Father has given all judgment to the Son (John 5:21–23). So as King and Judge in the most expanded meaning of these two words, Jesus has authority that cannot be overstated.

Christ as Lord and Master. We Christians have a confession of authority that unites us. The Christian gospel or message of faith concisely stated demands two things: (1) confession with the mouth that Jesus is Lord, (2) belief in the heart that God raised him from the dead (Rom. 10:9–10). The whole person is involved in this confession. To confess Jesus Christ as Lord means that he rules every aspect of our lives. He is our Authority, our "Boss," our Master. When sin deceives us and we transgress, we are denying our confession. Then Jesus is not ruling and he is not our authority. We have made a subtle shift. We ourselves have become the authority.

Paul tells of a day when every knee will bow at the mention of the person of Jesus and every tongue will confess that Jesus Christ is Lord, to the glory of God the Father (Phil. 2:9–10). This points to a universal recognition of Christ's authority. There will be no agnostics, no atheists. At present, freely, openly to declare Jesus to be Lord in the face of all opposition brings salvation. In the future day when the Lord is also Judge, the acknowledgment will be simply a statement of the way things are. In that situation it does not mean all men will be saved. When persons in day-by-day decisions rule God out of their lives and refuse to let him transform their whole persons, they have determined to be independent from God. Such people will in the day of judgment acknowledge that Christ *is* the authority, but God still gives them what they have wanted—their independence. The first death is a separation from the earthly body. The second death is separation from God. Such a separation is death, indeed.

Christ's exaltation. Peter asserts that Pentecost is the outcome of Jesus being exalted (to heaven) "by the right hand," "by the power of God," or "at the right hand of God"(RSV). He (Jesus) having "received from the Father the promise of the Holy Spirit has poured out this which you see and hear" (Acts 2:33). The ascension of Christ was his exaltation. The ascension also clarified Christ's authority. The powerful coming of the Holy Spirit upon Christ's followers showed that what Jesus had promised to them he brought about. In this experience, the living Christ, though highly exalted, was also powerfully present.

Pentecost was only the beginning of Christ's continuing redemptive activity. The writer of Hebrews describes Christ as being exalted above the heavens (7:26): "We have such a high priest, one who is seated at the right hand of the throne of the Majesty in heaven" (Heb. 8:1). The exalted Christ is also a priestly minister.

Christ's distinctive role as High Priest. Jesus, the Savior, functions as a high priest, "a minister in the sanctuary and true tent which is set up not by man but by the Lord" (Heb. 8:2, RSV). Christ's authority here is obvious in that he actively participates in the effects of his atoning death both in heaven and upon earth. The "heavenly sanctuary" is mentioned in Hebrews 9:11. Christ's own blood (life poured out for us) is the basis for his work in this heavenly sanctuary (9:12). Ceremonial cleansing was the outcome of the sacrifices under the first covenant (9:13), but Christ's atoning blood does more: it cleanses the conscience (9:14). The authoritative priest is the mediator of the New Covenant (9:15). His earthly and heavenly priestly action atones for sins under both covenants (9:15). Christ's authority is tied to the effectiveness of his saving work. He alone provides the remedy for man's alienation and sin.

Christ's relationship to law. Christ came not to destroy the law or the prophets but rather to fulfill them (Matt. 5:17). The expression "law or the prophets" covers the whole of the Old Testament. In what he did and taught, Jesus brought into operation all that the Old Testament promised.[7] This does not mean that sin is banished and all of its effects removed. But the Christ who came to fulfill the law has laid the basis, and transformed the lives of his people, so that the complete fulfillment of the promises is indicated by what has already begun.

The teaching of Jesus and the new covenant which he inaugurated brings a new lifestyle. Christians are to restore a brother who is overtaken in any tresspass (Gal. 6:1). They are to bear one another's crushing weights (Gal. 6:2a). In this manner they will fulfill completely the law of Christ (Gal. 6:2b). Christ's law is that of love (John 13:34–35). According to Jesus, on the two laws of loving God and one's neighbor, the whole of the Old Testament hangs (Matt. 22:37–40, Mark 14:29–31). Paul, in following Jesus' authority, turns law from legalism to attitude and action.

Christ's commands: comprehensive and compelling. In the great commission of Matthew 28:19–20, Jesus described what is involved in making disciples. After Jesus' followers go to all the nations, they are to *make disciples by baptizing* those who respond (baptism is a drama of repentance, conversion, and faith) and *by teaching* them (28:19–20). What were they to teach the new disciples? "Teaching them to observe all things as many things as *I have commanded* you" (v. 20). Jesus spoke from his own authority. He said that discipleship involves learning, commitment, and obedience.

Jesus laid down his life for those whom he loves (John 15:13). His disciples are in a loving relationship with him, *if they do the things he has commanded them* (John 15:14). Jesus does not call them servants but loving friends (15:15). When we do what Christ commands, we indicate a loving relationship with him and acknowledge Christ's authority.

During Jesus' life, he commanded not only people but also the physical elements. After Jesus stilled the storm on the sea of Galilee (Matt. 8:23–27, Mark 4:35–41, Luke 8:22–25), his fearful disciples began to marvel. They asked each other: "Who then is this one who commands even the winds and the water, and these elements obey him?" (Luke 8:25) Jesus' authority is extensive; he is not only the Christ of salvation but also the Christ of creation.

Jesus as the inaugurator of the New Covenant. During the Last Supper at Passover time, Jesus instituted the Lord's supper. The broken bread and the cup pointed to him and what he was to do. Of the cup Jesus said: "This cup is the new covenant [established] by means of my blood" (1 Cor. 11:25). Its contents were poured out on behalf of the disciples (Luke 22:20). Matthew speaks of the blood of the covenant poured out on account of many for remission of sins (26:28). At this supper, so close to death, Jesus' authority permeated all that he did. He was establishing a permanent basis by which God and man could come together.

Personal communication by word and deed. Christ's communication was not limited to verbal means. In his ministry in Galilee, he used three methods: "He was going about in the whole of Galilee, (1) teaching in their synagogues, (2) and preaching the gospel of the kingdom, (3) and healing every sickness and every malady among the people" (Matt. 4:23). Those who heard and observed all that he said and did concluded: "The Christ, whenever he comes, he will not do greater signs than this one has done, will he? No, he will not" (John 7:31). The diversity of Jesus' communication reenforced his authority.

The Authority of God's Servants in the New Testament

Delegation of authority is both explicitly stated and constantly assumed. Although some unwarranted inferences have been drawn from delegated authority (e.g., its transferral to later generations in a specific way and line), the cause of the Christian church is hurt when delegated authority is explained away.

The Authority of the Apostles or the Twelve. After Peter's great confession, he was given the keys of the kingdom of heaven (Matt. 16:19a). Whatever he bound upon earth, would have been bound in heaven; whatever he would have loosed upon earth, would have been loosed in heaven (Matt. 16:19b). What was said to Peter about binding and loosing was said to all of the apostles in Matthew 18:18.

Here is a transfer of authority. Joachim Jeremias points out that this is judicial. "It is the authority to pronounce judgment on unbelievers and to promise forgiveness to believers. In sum we may say that the power of the keys is authority in the dispersing of the word of grace and judgment." [8]

John's Gospel enlarges further upon this saying from Matthew. Jesus proclaimed "Peace" to the twelve. He then exclaimed: "Just as the Father has sent me, I also am sending you" (John 20:21, cf. 17:18). With this delegated authority and with the Holy Spirit's presence, the disciples could declare the basis for the forgiveness of sins or the reason for the retention of sins. So although authority is delegated, the ultimate authority is God the Father who sent Christ, and Christ himself, who sent his disciples.

The authority of the Apostle Paul. Paul would be the last one to say that authority lay inherently in him (2 Cor. 4:7). He insists that the extraordinary quality of the power belongs to God and not to God's servants.

Paul's true authority lay in what God gave to him. The gospel proclaimed as good tidings by Paul was not *according to* man, it was not *received from* man by way of tradition, it *was not taught* to Paul by some authority like Gamaliel. Rather, the gospel came to Paul by revelation. This revelation was given by Jesus Christ (Gal. 11:11–12). The gospel has authority because of the One who gave it.

Further, Paul became a *minister (diakonos)* of this gospel (Col. 1:23). The gospel was good news to the Jews first and also to the Greeks or Gentiles (Rom. 1:16). Since God called Paul to be the apostle to the Gentiles, he extolled or magnified his *ministry* (Rom. 11:13). Summarizing this ministry, Paul emphasized the grace given to him by God to be a minister. Paul used priestly terms. The purpose of this grace was that Paul might be a minister *(leitourgon)* of Christ Jesus, ministering as a priest *(hierougounta)* the gospel of God, that the offering *(prosphora)* that consists of the Gentiles might be acceptable because it has been consecrated *(hēgiasmenē)* by the Holy Spirit (Rom. 15:16). Paul's authority is expressed in this kind of ministry that God gave him and that he so earnestly and eagerly carried out. His words here show the deep sense of responsibility Paul had in living up to the demands of his task. Delegated authority for Paul was a sacred trust.

Paul's collection for the poverty-stricken saints at Jerusalem came through a careful use of his authority (Rom. 15:25–29; 1 Cor. 16:1; 2 Cor. 8–9). Paul's fellow workers had no doubt about his authority and leadership. Titus knew that his job on Crete was to appoint elders, city by city, as Paul commanded (Tit. 1:5).

Paul spoke of his ministry as involving not only the gospel but also *the new covenant.* Paul's fitness, capability, qualifications were from God (2 Cor. 3:5). Paul and his fellow workers were empowered, made sufficient to be ministers *(diakonous)* of a new covenant. This new covenant does not belong to a written, legalistic code but belongs to the Spirit. The written legalistic code kills, but the Spirit gives life (2 Cor. 3:6). God enhances the authority of the ministers, and the character of the new covenant also enhances their authority. The new covenant showed Paul's ministry to be that of the Spirit, of righteousness and abiding glory.

Paul was a communicator for God in a way that few men have been. He said he was thankful that the Thessalonians received God's word of preaching from him, not as the word of men but as it truly is the word of God (1 Thess. 2:13). Paul's *preached word* was the word of God. Similarly Paul told the Corinthians that the Spirit of God enabled him to *know* things that were graciously granted to him by God (Paul is speaking about his ministry in Corinth). "Which things also we are speaking, not in words taught of human wisdom but in words taught of the Spirit interpreting spiritual things to spiritual men" (1 Cor. 2:13). Paul's spoken word involved what was taught by the Spirit. Paul was a teacher as well as a preacher (see 1 Tim. 2:7; 2 Tim. 1:10–11). The passage in 2 Timothy 1:11 speaks of a threefold appointment: "I was appointed (1) a preacher or herald, (2) an apostle, and (3) a teacher." These are offices with authority. Paul's authority made an impact because of the content of his preaching, his teaching, and all that was involved in his apostleship.

The awareness of authority of this kind gave Paul a sense of urgency. "Him [Christ] we *are proclaiming, admonishing* every man, *teaching* every man, that we might present every man complete in Christ" (Col. 1:28).

Importance of Biblical Authority for Today

Biblical authority is important for us today because from the Bible we derive all the truths that we need to live effectively for God in our world.

The Bible *inherently* has authority. Beethoven's Ninth Symphony *inherently* has musical authority when the score lies on the stand before the orchestra conductor. But when the score becomes part of the musicians themselves and they play all of their parts together, then the reality of the *inherent authority* comes across. So it is with the contents of the Bible.

Think of the world of music without the printing press. Even if the conductor had the autograph and all musicians had carefully made hand-written copies, the rehearsal would be much harder than it is now! Nevertheless, in that situation the inherent authority of great music would always ring out in the concert.

Now look at our inerrancy controversies. So often we silently import a printing press mentality into all of our discussions (remember, type printing began in the 1450s). Printing and then later the use of typewriters have strongly influenced our approach to composition. Printing has given us maps and atlases

that have influenced our view of history and geography. Imagine mathematics without printing or Arabic numerals. As we
have seen, people in biblical times knew only of scrolls. Even
the book form or codex came in after New Testament times. But
it was the printing press that established books and bookbinding.
The technological advances of the last five hundred years make
it easy for all of us to come face to face with the true authority
of the Bible. But let us not assume that the Bible was written in
the atmosphere of modern technology. The biblical truths shine
out all the more wondrously when we think of the atmosphere
in which they were written.

How did these truths have authority in their biblical setting?
Looking at the contents of the Bible, we sense authority as we
perceive *the interaction* of God with his chosen servants, with
his people, and with Christ. We also sense authority when we
perceive *the interaction* of Christ with God, with his chosen
servants, and with his people. The various linguistic expressions
and categories highlight this interaction. The material is vast
and extensive. In this chapter we have examined only a few
examples. These relationships are *like a magnetic field of force*
which affects everything that comes within the field.[9] God, his
servants, Christ, Christ's servants, and the people of God in
various incidents and teachings radiate authority as a magnet
extends its field in truths that direct our steps and thoughts.
Other materials in the Bible—such as Ecclesiastes, where the
writer empirically tests out life under the sun and declares its
vanity—are touched by this magnetic field of force, by this
radiating authority. They, too, have authority. In the perspective
of a God who acts, discloses truth, and brings about complete
redemption, "the vanity theme" of Ecclesiastes and the deep
pessimism of parts of Job clearly show how essential are the
distinctive truths of revelation. Man does not live by bread
alone. The Bible testifies eloquently that when man tries to live
without God, life becomes increasingly dark.

How do the truths of the Bible have authority for us today?
When by sound interpretation we make proper application of

the contents, the Bible radiates authority. This word with its truths is a lamp to our feet and a light to our paths (Ps. 119:105). Men may still reject these truths. They may object that the true message from God is only human opinion. However, the real objection often is not with *the form* of the message but rather with *the response* that the message demands. We who believe in the authority of the Bible need to dedicate ourselves to living out these truths. "Consecrate them in the sphere of your truth; your word or message is truth" (John 17:17).

IS "SCRIPTURE ALONE"
THE ESSENCE OF CHRISTIANITY?

by Bernard Ramm

Bernard Ramm is Professor of Theology at Eastern Baptist Seminary in Philadelphia, Pennsylvania. He has also held professorships at Los Angeles Baptist Seminary, the Bible Institute of Los Angeles, Bethel College and Seminary (St. Paul, Minnesota), Baylor University (Waco, Texas), and California Baptist Seminary (Covina). Dr. Ramm is author of eighteen books, among them Hermeneutics *(Baker, 1971),* The God Who Makes a Difference *(Word, 1972), and* The Evangelical Heritage *(Word, 1973). He has also written more than 100 articles for a variety of theological journals and Christian periodicals. He is a member of the President's Board of Associates of Bethel College and Seminary, a member of the American Academy of Religion, and an Honorary Fellow of the American Scientific Foundation. Dr. Ramm holds the A.B. degree from the University of Washington, B.D. from Eastern Baptist Seminary, M.A. and Ph.D. from the University of Southern California, and has done post-graduate work at Basel and at the Near East School of Theology. In September 1977 Dr. Ramm will become Theologian-in-Residence, First Baptist Church of Modesto, California, and Professor of Christianity at Simpson College, Modesto campus.*

MORE THAN A century ago, the first of two books with almost identical titles was published in Germany. Ludwig Feuerbach wrote *Wesen des Christentums* in 1841, and later Adolph Harnack published *Das Wesen des Christentums* in 1900.

The German word *Wesen* is a strong one. It means the essence of something, the real spirit or burden of a treatise, the heart of the matter. *Christentum* means Christianity. Hence these books were asking: What is the essence of Christianity? Boiled down to absolute basics what does Christianity intend to mean? Apart from all the externals what is at the heart of Christianity?

Sola scriptura is a phrase from the Reformation. It meant that in theological disputation, especially with Roman Catholic theologians, the Scriptures were the sole and final authority. This principle was framed to counter the Roman Catholic view of a divine tradition.

Is sola scriptura *the* Wesen *of Christianity?*

We commonly date the beginning of liberal theology with Schleiermacher's publication of his *Speeches* (*Reden*) in 1799. The development of higher criticism during this period led

in many instances to a marriage of higher critical views of
Scripture with liberal theology.

Both the liberal theology of Schleiermacher and the use of
higher criticism grew rapidly in favor, spreading eventually into
all the Christian world. The history of that movement need not
be repeated in detail here. But orthodox or evangelical theologians recognized that a real battle was emerging. It was to be a
battle over the *Wesen* of Christianity. One of its most important decisions concerned the strategy to be adopted by the
historic theologians for combating the spread of liberal theology and higher criticism in the Christian church and in Christian
schools.

The Hodge-Warfield Strategy

As the debate was beginning to heat up in America a famous
essay appeared, in *The Presbyterian Review,* "Inspiration,"
written by A. A. Hodge and B. B. Warfield, both of Princeton
Theological Seminary (7:225–260, April, 1881). The essay
did not say in so many words that it was an expression of a
strategy to combat higher criticism and liberalism in the church,
but this is what it amounted to. And it is important in that in
recent years its strategy, with some significant modifications, has
been urged afresh as the strategy for all evangelicals in the
jungle of contemporary theology. (See "Misplaced battle lines,"
my review of Harold Lindsell's *The Battle for the Bible* in *The
Reformed Journal* [July-August, 1976] for a discussion of one
such proposal.)

The position of the Hodge-Warfield essay was that one's view
of Holy Scripture is at the heart of the controversy. Therefore
it set out to describe that view of Holy Scripture which would
be the line of attack and provide the strategy for combat against
liberalism and higher criticism. The view of Scripture can be
stated in five theses: (1) Holy Scripture is plenarily or fully inspired; (2) Holy Scripture is verbally inspired; (3) Holy Scripture is inerrant in all matters upon which it touches; (4) in that

we do not have the original copies of the books of Scripture we must be aware that certain problems or discrepancies urged against Scripture might not be in the original text; and (5) by the proper use of the historical-critical method of biblical interpretation discrepancies can be resolved or else shown to have enough ambiguity that they do not constitute a threat to the inerrancy of Scripture.

The essay is in many ways an amazing document. At the same time that it makes some very high claims for the completely errorless character of Scripture it also makes unusual concessions to the humanity and historicity of the Scriptures. It will assert on one page that Scripture is absolutely without error and on another that it is the *intention* of the author which determines what is meant by inerrancy. Or it will affirm that the Scripture does not intend a perfection in its statements but rather an accuracy which suits its purposes (e.g., Old Testament citations in the New Testament need not be exact renditions of the Old Testament text). It was this give-and-take which led the great Scottish evangelical James Orr to say that, although the essay denied any error in Scripture, its many qualifications about what constituted an error offered tacit admission that there were some.

There were two things which A. A. Hodge and B. B. Warfield, as scholars with much learning, were careful not to say, and this is very important for what follows: (1) They did not say that inspiration was the first and foremost doctrine of the Christian faith but the last doctrine of the faith; that is, it was not the lead-premise of theology but the final conclusion to which Christian theology leads us. (2) They did not say that Christian doctrines rested upon a doctrine of inspiration for their substantiation; rather, they said that Christianity was true independently of any theory of inspiration, and its great doctrines were believable within themselves.

The reader can judge from the following the measure of extreme statement found in the essay. These phrases occur on the pages indicated: "absolutely infallible," (226); "absolutely errorless," (227); "without error of facts or doctrines," (228); "errorless expression," (231); "an errorless record," (232); "infallible in its verbal expression," (234); "absolute truthfulness," (236); "errorless infallibility of the words," (240); errorless infallibility of all Scriptural affirmations," (241); and "absolute freedom from error of its statements," (243).

Any subjects touched upon in teaching doctrine are also statements which are inerrant such as statements about history, natural history, ethnology, archaeology, geography, or natural science (236). Statements about spiritual doctrine or duty, physical or historical fact, psychological or philosophical principle are also without error (238).

From the other writings of Warfield in particular, it would be impossible to say that he identified the *Wesen* of Christianity with his view of Holy Scripture. He was enough of a historian of theology to avoid saying that. The "inspiration" article was an essay in strategy. However, among current followers of the so-called Warfield position there have been certain shifts away from the original strategic stance of the essay. One's doctrine of Scripture has become now the first and most important doctrine, one's theory of the *Wesen* of Christianity, so that all other doctrines have validity now only as they are part of the inerrant Scripture. Thus evangelical teachers, or evangelical schools or evangelical movements, can be judged as to whether or not they are true to the *Wesen* of Christianity by their theory of inspiration. It can be stated even more directly: an evangelical has made a theory of inspiration the *Wesen* of Christianity if he assumes that the most important doctrine in a man's theology, and most revelatory of the entire range of his theological thought, is his theology of inspiration.

A Variety of Historical Views

Such a stance must be viewed as a theological oddity for the following reasons:

1. To make one certain theory of inspiration the *Wesen* of Christianity reduces to a very small group the number of people really true to Christianity. The truth is that there are many doctrines of inspiration, as I can corroborate from having read a number of essays on "the church doctrine of inspiration." Further substantiation is to be found in Bruce Vawter's history of the doctrine, *Biblical Inspiration* (1972), in the series called *Theological Resources.* We may find recurring themes or common emphases, but to affirm that there is one highly specialized theory of inspiration which runs unbroken through church history is an argument that cannot be maintained. And if that cannot be maintained it makes it very difficult to presume, from the standpoint of historical theology, that the Hodge-Warfield position is the one church doctrine.

2. It is true that the Reformers and their immediate followers had commented on the inspiration of Scripture. But this discussion was always within the context of that element in Scripture wherein it is divine, or wherein it is the Word of God. Different words were used and different emphases were made but the structure is the same.

Luther had a Christological understanding of Scripture. For him it is the unique Christ-bearing of Scripture which is its peculiar divine element. Calvin, on the other hand, says it is the majesty in Scripture wherein we discover that it is the Word of God. There must not only be a doctrine of inspiration but some special *indicium* which by the power of the Spirit reveals Scripture to be the Word of God. And that quality Calvin called the majesty of Scripture.

Other writers expressed the divinity of Scripture in that it was "worthy of belief," meaning that Scripture is the Word of God in and of itself. It bears its own "Word-of-Godness," to use an awkward expression. Others used the word *autopistia*, which meant self-credible, capable of verifying itself as the Word of God.

No formal doctrine of Scripture is self-contained. Therefore to invest the *Wesen* of Christianity in a formal view of its inspiration does not do justice to the Scriptures, nor was it the stance of the Reformers.

God's Acts in History Preceded Their Being Written

3. All the doctrines based on events in history then rest for their reality in the bed of history, whether they are ever recorded or not. To say that we know these doctrines only in virtue of Scripture is to confuse the *ordo essendi* (how a given subject matter is constituted) with the *ordo cognoscendi* (how the subject matter is known or learned). It is precisely these doctrines relating historical events which do form so much of the *Wesen* of Christianity. Christ was crucified for our sins whether that was ever recorded in a book or not; Christ rose from the dead whether that ever be made a topic of written testimony.

To make a certain view of Scripture the *Wesen* of Christianity means that all such doctrines implied in the above paragraph are second order doctrines. For if the *Wesen* of Christianity is a certain theory of inspiration then all doctrines are only as good as our theory of inspiration is. This step the Hodge-Warfield essay did not take. It had too much of a sense of historical theology and of the real *Wesen* of Christianity.

4. Cults and sects usually have a doctrine of inspiration similar to that found in the later Hodge-Warfield tradition. If a certain view of Scripture is the *Wesen* of Christianity, and cultists and sectarians believe that view of Scripture, by logic we are compelled to admit that they are evangelicals.

Conversely, if a theologian accepts all the great affirmations we usually associate with the title evangelical but has a view of inspiration divergent from his critic, then his entire theology is suspect and by definition he is not an evangelical. Again this leads to the oddity that in theology some person of mediocre mind and education is to be trusted, but a man with a brilliant mind and evangelical faith like Thomas Torrance is suspect because his view of Scripture is essentially Barthian. But we can do no better than this in theology if we identify the *Wesen* of Christianity with a particular view of inspiration.

The Use of Scripture More Important Than Theory

5. The effort to make the doctrine of inspiration the *Wesen* of Christianity runs into serious trouble from another direction. Perhaps far more fundamental than a theory of the inspiration of the Scriptures is how a theologian uses Holy Scripture. There are some excellent studies on this subject. For example, Klaus Reinhardt has written a large volume, *Der Dogmatische Schriftgebrauch,* or *The Use of Scripture in Dogma* (the book, published in 1970, is available only in German at this time). In the fine print we are told that it is occupied with views of Christology among Catholic and Protestant theologians from the Enlightenment to the present. It is over five hundred pages of sustained research. A smaller but similar kind of book, in English, is *The Uses of Scripture in Recent Theology* by D. H. Kelsey (1975).

Reading these works leads one to the conclusion that there is no absolute correlation between what a theologian thinks about Scripture and how he uses it. Many of the church fathers held substantial views of the inspiration of Scripture, but the entire evangelical camp would gag on their allegorical interpretations. On the other hand, men like Otto Piper and Oscar Cullmann, whose views of Scripture are substandard, according to many evangelicals, manage to write some very solid theology.

As contrary to evangelical thought as Barth's understanding of the concept of inspiration may be, no serious student of theology can deny that some of the greatest pages on biblical theology in this century were written by Barth in his *Church Dogmatics.*

We should not be caught in a position where our understanding of the *Wesen* of Christianity forces us to accept trashy theology, substandard by all academic criteria, as evangelical, and to brand as nonevangelical some great biblical theology. But if we make a particular view of Scripture the *Wesen* of Christianity there is no escape from such conclusions.

The "Bible-Only" Mentality

6. The notion of a theory of inspiration being the *Wesen* of Christianity is rightly suspect of coming from a "Bible-only" mentality.

Sola scriptura did not affirm that, with reference to the writing of theology, all knowledge other than biblical knowledge is unnecessary. It meant that, when it came to decision-making in controversy, the appeal to Scripture was the highest appeal possible, and that, where Scripture spoke on a point, the verdict of Scripture was final. The Bible-only mentality confuses the *sola scriptura* of the Reformation with criteria of theological scholarship. The Bible-only mentality makes the record of revelation more primordial than the original revelation; it makes the history Scripture reports of second order to the scriptural report. The Bible-only mentality in principle reduces theology to the simplicities of proof-texting theological convictions.

Finally, a Bible-only mentality virtually equates spiritual reality with the text of Scripture itself, whereas the Scripture is a pointer to or a witness to that reality.

But theological craftsmanship cannot be so limited. If we wish to know how to spell a word in theology, we use a dictionary. If we want information about some aspect of biblical geography, we turn to a book of geography. If we want the whole picture of Pilate we must use extra-biblical sources. To understand, as much as it is humanly possible, the total context of a biblical word and its historical development we may well use the famous Kittel's *Theological Dictionary of the New Testament* (10 vols.).

There is a difference between being biblical and biblicistic (i.e., employing the Bible-only mentality). There is a difference between honoring *sola scriptura* and bibliolatry (the excess veneration of Scripture). There is a difference between a Christian view of Scripture and a Muslim view of Scripture. The

Muslims believe that the earthly *Qu'ran* is a perfect copy of an actual *Qu'ran* in Paradise. Hence there is in theory no historical criticism and no textual criticism of the *Qu'ran*. On more than one occasion it has been pointed out that the Bible-only view of Scripture is very much like the Muslim view of Scripture. The Christian view of Scripture is that there is a human and histori- cal dimension to Scripture and therefore biblical criticism and textual criticism are necessary studies for the proper understand- ing of Scripture.

But this is not all. Scripture is not the totality of all God has said and done in this world. Scripture is that part of revelation and history specially chosen for the life of the people of God through centuries. *Sola scriptura* means that the canon of Scrip- ture is the final authority in the church; it does not claim to be the record of all God has said and done.

Hence our concept of the essence, the *Wesen,* of Christianity must have an eye open to some larger considerations. Such a *Wesen* will then be in harmony with the considerations every theologian must make himself aware of in order to have a proper concept of the Scriptures themselves.

Inspiration in the Context of a Covenant Community

1. The first matter we have in mind is the comprehensive nature of revelation. G. Vos writes somewhat ponderously of the different species of divine revelation in his work *Biblical Theol- ogy.* He does, however, force us to see that the range of divine revelation must be larger than what we have in Holy Scripture. The first statement within Scripture concerning the process of writing occurs in Exodus. We do not know how many centuries or millennia are implied by the Book of Genesis, but it is cer- tainly fair to say that there must have been much more revela- tory work of God in that time span than is recorded there. The first eleven chapters themselves are an enormous compaction of history.

2. Although God's Word comes to individuals here and there, it is addressed to a larger circle. We may think of clans

in the patriarchal period, a nation at the time of the prophets, and the church in the New Testament. In fact, the notion of revelation is correlative to that of a people of God. Revelation and inspiration in this context intend to be public documents. Whether it be revelation or inspiration or *sola scriptura,* the context is always a people of God.

In his survey of the history of the doctrine of inspiration (*Biblical Inspiration*), Bruce Vawter is so impressed by the correlation of inspiration and a people of God that he proposes a new concept of inspiration. He proposes that inspiration be understood as a grace of the whole people of God. While I do not think that can really be done, it does underline the truth that revelation and inspiration are concepts which are alive in a very special group of people, either Israel or the church. Certainly in some instances the prophet stands outside the community and challenges the whole people of God, and that kind of prophetic challenge must never be cut short. But the more normal pattern is the prophetic speaking occurring within the context of the people of God.

3. One of the products of modern biblical scholarship is a thorough understanding of the notion of covenant and its centrality to a biblical way of thinking. God's people are also God's covenantal people. A covenantal relationship between God and man is different from a contractual relationship. It is God's sovereignty and grace which brings him into covenantal relationship with his people; hence revelation and inspiration occur within a covenantal community and are part of a covenantal understanding of God and Israel or God and the church. Or we may express it this way: revelation and inspiration occur within a covenantal people of God and therefore must be understood within the context of a covenant.

The Significance of Christian Tradition

4. It has been a twisted road for biblical scholars to recover the concept of tradition in its healthy sense. Our Lord had his

conflict with the Jews of his time and their traditions (Matt. 15:6). Paul too found himself in conflict with the traditions of his times (Col. 2:8). The conflict of church tradition and the authority of Scripture resulted in the Reformers' affirmation of *sola scriptura*.

More patient research in the matter of tradition has brought to the surface the good side of the concept. Paul himself uses the language of tradition in a good sense (1 Cor. 11:23, 15:3). Both Roman Catholic and Protestant scholars have been coming closer and closer in a newer and better notion of tradition on both sides. For example, they agree that much of the revelation given in the period of time contained in the Book of Genesis must have been carried on as tradition. When Moses talked with the elders of Israel (in Exodus) apparently the revelations made to the patriarchs had been carried on for centuries by tradition. In the Christian period the bridge between Christ and the written documents of the New Testament was certainly tradition.

The *sola scriptura* of the Reformers did not mean a total rejection of tradition. It meant that only Scripture had the final word on a subject. The use by the Reformers of the writings of the Fathers shows how deeply they were nourished by Christian tradition.

The very strong case for tradition made by the Eastern church cannot be easily dismissed. It insists that the context of meaning of the New Testament is church tradition. If we reject church tradition we have no idea what the New Testament is attempting to communicate.

There is no question that the great majority of American evangelicals are not happy to have such a large weight given to tradition. Even so, the point of the Eastern church is significant. Can we so completely ignore tradition and still make sense out of the New Testament? Might we not be heirs of tradition in such a manner that we are not aware of it? However we vote on this issue, it remains true that scholars no longer can talk about Scripture and totally ignore tradition.

If this is a question in the history of the church it is no question with Old Testament scholars today. Their researches have shown how rich a role the concept of tradition has played in the growth of the Old Testament.

William Chillingworth (1602–1644) is famous for his assertion that "the Bible only is the religion of Protestants." If this was simply another way of affirming *sola scriptura* there is no debate with Chillingworth. And historically it appears that this is the sense in which the famous words were uttered. But if he was asserting that the *Wesen* of Christianity is the Scriptures and only the Scriptures, then we must say, to the contrary, that the religion of Protestants must be more comprehensive (cf. *sola gratia, sola fide, sola Christus*).

5. The New Testament presents Christ as delivering his commission to the apostles, who in turn founded the church and began the writing of the New Testament. There is also the promise that they would be given the Holy Spirit in a special fullness. But we also learn that from the day of Pentecost onward the church had a sacramental life. Although this is recorded in the Book of Acts, the sacramental life of the church had been going on long before the New Testament was written. Our point does not depend on any sacramental theology. It depends on the assertion that the early church did baptize and did share in the Lord's Supper. In the understanding of the theology of the sacraments we certainly call upon *sola scriptura*. But that does not erase the fact that we could have an apostolic succession of the sacraments. Or let us put it another way: (1) to understand the place of sacraments in the life of the church we must have recourse to all sources; (2) but in determining the theology of the sacraments we turn to Scripture. Or we may also say that our historical understanding of Christianity and our appeal to *sola scriptura* are not mutually exclusive.

The Influence of the Invention of Printing

6. The penchant for a Bible-only Christianity runs into a problem which forces us to be more comprehensive in our

understanding of the gospel, the church, faith and the believer. In a class in theology we were discussing the significance of the origin of the printing press in the middle of the fifteenth century. I had just pointed out that the publication of Luther's German translation of the Scriptures marked the first time in the history of the church that all Christians who had the relatively small sum of money necessary could buy their own copies of Scripture.

One of the students looked more and more distressed as the lecture progressed. When he could contain himself no longer, he blurted out his question: "If it was not until the time of printing that the ordinary Christian could have his own copy of Holy Scripture, where were all the true Christians before the printing of Scripture?"

I use this personal experience to make my point because the issue was put so clearly by the student in the context of the lecture. The reason the student was disturbed was that he had a Bible-only mentality. If a Christian could not have his own Scripture until the time of printing and its translation into modern languages, then the kind of Christianity the Bible-only mentality accepts could not have existed until the sixteenth century. It also follows that the previous fifteen centuries were somehow lost centuries, and it was this concept of so many lost centuries which was distressing the student.

My reply was something like this: In theology our appeal is to *sola scriptura*. The early church did have the Old Testament and began to assemble the New Testament into a canon in the second century. Hence theologians could always be held to *sola scriptura*.

But if copies of the Holy Scripture were rare because of the expensive cost of reproduction by hand-copying then there must have been other valid sources through which the laymen could know the contents of the Christian faith. Such may be: (1) the preaching of the bishop in the early church who did have his Scriptures and did preach from them could then impart biblical knowledge to the laity through preaching; (2) the sacraments and the liturgy which used biblical themes, biblical personalities, and quotations from Scripture so that solid biblical truth could be learned indirectly from sacraments and liturgy; (3) church architecture, decorations within a church, and other forms of Christian art which reflected biblical themes and materials.

This is not an exhaustive list but it does show how the millions of Christians of both the Western and Eastern churches could have had a substantial understanding of the Christian faith prior to the invention of printing. And if one has such a perspective on the whole history of the church he need not be caught in the logical box to which the Bible-only mentality leads.

The previous material may appear to be a digression but it is meant to express a conviction. I strongly believe that the current effort to make a certain doctrine of Scripture the *Wesen* of Christianity represents a Bible-only mentality which cannot be supported because it is so narrow that it becomes self-defeating.

Summary

For purposes of clarification we wish to sum up the theses we have been defending:

1. There is no questioning of the *sola scriptura* in theology. Scripture is the supreme and final authority in theological decision-making.

2. One's views of revelation, inspiration, and interpretation are important. They do implicate each other. Our discussion rather has been whether a certain view of inspiration could stand as the *Wesen* of Christianity. We have in no manner suggested that matters of revelation, inspiration, and interpretation are unimportant in theology.

3. We have maintained that the manner in which some evangelicals are speaking of their view of inspiration asserts that a certain view of inspiration (usually the one in the Hodge-Warfield essay) constitutes the *Wesen* of Christianity. The evidence for this is that such evangelicals use their doctrine of inspiration in such a way that it becomes, for them, the *Wesen* of Christianity. If the integrity of other evangelicals, evangelical schools, or evangelical movements are assessed by their view of

inspiration, then, for them, inspiration has become the *Wesen* of Christianity. This is especially evident when an evangelical's total theological stance is written off because he does not think a popular doctrine of inspiration is the right one, or if he thinks that the doctrine of inspiration is not the *Wesen* of Christianity.

4. We have tried to show that there is a difference between a Bible-only mentality which is limited and limiting and a healthy strong, theological stance on *sola scriptura*. The latter is in total accord with the theology of the Reformers and is compatible with a genuinely contemporary evangelical theological scholarship.

THE PASTOR AS A
BIBLICAL CHRISTIAN

by Earl Palmer

Earl F. Palmer is Senior Pastor of First Presbyterian Church of Berkeley, California. Before assuming that position, he served the Union Church of Manila, Philippines, as Pastor, and prior to that time was Minister to Students at University Presbyterian Church in Seattle, Washington. Rev. Palmer, who has traveled extensively throughout Europe, the Middle and Far East, Russia, and many other countries, is author of Salvation by Surprise: Studies in the Book of Romans *(Word, 1975) and* Love Has Its Reasons: An Inquiry into New Testament Love *(Word, 1977). Dr. Palmer holds the B.A. degree from the University of California (Berkeley), and the B.D. from Princeton Theological Seminary.*

I WAS AN UNDERGRADUATE at Berkeley when the Bible first became a book I really wanted to read. I lived in a large co-op called Barrington Hall, and it was there in a weekly student-led Bible discussion group that the random pieces of my world view came together. It was my discovery of the Jesus Christ of the Bible that made the difference for me, because Jesus Christ as Lord integrated the parts into a new whole. He resolved a journey that had begun in my childhood and he called me into a growing lifelong adventure called the Christian life. It seems to me that when I agreed to Jesus Christ as Lord, I was granted, along with every other Christian, a fourfold mandate: (1) first we are called to grow in our relationship with God himself, Father, Son, Holy Spirit (Rom. 1:1–6); (2) we are commanded to *love* our neighbor by word and action (1 John 4); (3) we are commanded to share the message of the Good News that Jesus Christ is the Savior and the Lord (Matt. 28); (4) we are commanded to build up the body of Christ, which is the church, so that the first three mandates may be fulfilled in the whole world (Eph. 4).

The authority for each mandate is the same: Jesus Christ who himself is the word of God and the work of God. We know the meaning of love because of the historical event in which God's love has broken through as concrete and real. Therefore, the Christian is challenged to love, not out of emptiness, but be-

127

cause Jesus Christ first loved us. Love is not an energy or mood; it is word and event inseparably united in Jesus Christ.

Our challenge to share the message of the gospel also has derived from its single source, which is Jesus Christ himself and the historical witness to him—the Bible. The message Christians have to share is not a sentiment or experience. It is not our love, our faith, our hope. It is not a dynamic twentieth-century strategy for peace and justice. We are not the gospel; nor are the forces of history the gospel. The gospel is about Jesus Christ, his love, his reign.

"Every verse of the Gospels tells us that the origin of Christianity is not the kerygma, not the resurrection experience of the disciples, not the Christ idea, but an historical event, to wit, the appearance of the man Jesus of Nazareth,"[1] declares Joachim Jeremias.

Who is this Jesus Christ? He is the Jesus of history to whom the Bible bears witness in the Old Testament by its history and expectation, and in the New Testament in its fulfillment. We do not know an eternal mystical Christ of faith apart from the concrete Jesus of the first century. Christian theology cannot endorse an ethics which is only conceptual and theoretical; so we cannot agree to a Christology that is ideological or spiritualized. The cornerstone of Christian theology and its most radical cutting edge is the affirmation of the fact that the "Word became flesh" (John 1). If we agree that this is indeed the Jesus Christ in whom we trust and must obey, then we have joined ourselves to the Bible.

Biblical Authority in Conversion

The Bible is the "evidence of the self-evidence"[2] of God himself. It receives its authority in borrowed fashion from its center, who is Jesus Christ. We can understand in practical terms what this means when we reflect personally upon how we ourselves became Christians. Someone—perhaps many people in different ways—turned our attention to consider the person of Christ himself. We read and heard of him within the historical witness of the New Testament to his person and work. Perhaps we began our journey with serious reservations, even skeptically, not at all impressed by the importance of the Bible. We nevertheless listened to its accounts. Matthew, whoever he is, we said to ourselves, tells about Jesus. Mark, Luke, and John also tell of Jesus' works, his ministry, his death and his victory. Paul writes letters to pockets of believers throughout the first-century world, and in that correspondence even more of the parts of the puzzle come together of who the person Jesus Christ is.

Finally, whether gradually or quickly, the New Testament Jesus won us to himself. He gained our respect and our faith. Our trust in the witness to him was confirmed to us by the Holy Spirit, and we became Christians. As believers we were made a part of the Body of Christ, and the fourfold mandate was ours.

Biblical Authority over Our Experience

The pastor, like every Christian, has been granted the same mandates with neither less nor greater imperative. The one difference is that the pastor has been ordained by the community of believers to bear special responsibility as a teacher of the message of the gospel and to be an enabler of the whole people of God in fulfilling their ministries in the world. It is this ordination to teach the gospel and to encourage the gifts of the whole body that we now want to consider in some depth.

Our first question is theologically crucial and intensely existential as well. Where does the pastor find the ingredient themes and content for the sermon to be preached at Sunday worship? What is the source for the teaching? Or to put the question in theological perspective: what is the authority for the message of the pastor, or the Young Life leader at a Tuesday evening club meeting, or the seminary professor's lecture on the Third Article of the Westminster Confession; or for that matter for any Christian as he or she seeks to understand and share the meaning of the Christian gospel?

The answer is not as simple as we might suppose! Consider

this possibility: A Christian has experienced with new and fresh reality the full impact of God's grace. The experience is dramatically real and immediate. There is no question in the mind of the Christian that the experience has been granted as a gift from God. He or she is able to point to signs of changed attitudes and lifestyle as proof of God's working. Shall we preach this experience? Is perhaps this very experience the message we have to affirm on Sunday or Tuesday evening? Is not this contemporary work of the Holy Spirit in the lives of God's people the most relevant message for our time? Or add a further possibility: What of the even greater spiritual breakthroughs that some Christians have experienced—visions, dreams, angels? Many would insist that certainly these gifts of the Holy Spirit deserve to be affirmed and proclaimed so that the world may be humbled by such signs and the Christians encouraged. What should be our reply to these possibilities?

For visions and for all of the experiences of God's grace we are grateful, but they are not the source of our message. We do not proclaim them as if they were the Good News. What we must proclaim is the gospel of Jesus Christ. The authoritative witness to that gospel is only the Bible. This means that the authority for the church is not the church, not the existential experiences of the Christians, not the challenging new visions of spiritual leaders, not the revolutionary imperatives of each new era, not the safe *status quo* priorities of the present.

The warm and personal endorsements of the Good News that come from our own experiences of the love of God are important twentieth-century witnesses to the timelessness of the reign of Christ, but they lack any binding authority in themselves. In an ironic sense the same observation may be made of the moral tragedies of life, the profound failures that are the result of human sin. These also are twentieth-century signposts which cry out the need of humanity for "total help to meet total need" (Karl Barth), and they demand a salvation that only Jesus Christ grants. But neither the positive experiences of the faithful, nor the negative rejection of a world separate and confused, have in themselves any binding authority over life. Therefore, they are not the content of the Message. For this reason we must reject as false any doctrine which teaches that the Holy Spirit continues to reveal new authoritative doctrines to the church. Jesus promised: "The Holy Spirit, whom the Father will send in my name, he will teach you all things, and bring to your remembrance all that I have said to you" (John 14:26).

John Calvin put it this way in his discussion of the doctrine of the Holy Spirit: "The whole of it comes to this; the Holy Spirit is the bond by which Christ binds us to Himself."[3] Paul prescribes precisely the same testing principle for the Colossian Christians when he warns them against the lofty visions and spiritual breakthroughs that certain members of the Colossian church had evidently made the basis for new authoritative teachings. Paul tells us that every doctrine must be tested by its relationship to the true center, which is God's Speech once and for all in Jesus Christ (Col. 2).

The early church, by its agreement upon the canon of Holy Scripture, interpreted Paul's testing principle as follows: All doctrine must be tested by its submission to the historical witness that surrounds Jesus Christ, namely, the Bible, consisting of the Old Testament and the New Testament. As we trust in Jesus Christ, we trust in the witness to him. We have been convinced by the Holy Spirit of the Jesus Christ we met in the biblical witness to him. The church's doctrine of the inspiration of the Scriptures rests on the belief that the Holy Spirit has preserved the faithfulness and trustworthiness of the documents and that the Holy Scriptures are those books God wants us to have. They point us faithfully to the center.

The Bible derives its authority in the following fashion: As the historic Jesus of Nazareth is the only Redeemer and the Good News is complete in him, therefore there are no hidden new gospels to be found or revealed. This conviction of the total sufficiency of Jesus Christ underlies the meaning of the doctrine of the infallibility of the Bible. By that doctrine we agree that only the one word which has been spoken in word and work—

Jesus Christ himself—shall have final binding authority over our lives and our doctrines.

Every new doctrinal statement, therefore, must be tested by that biblical witness. Every Christian doctrine, therefore, should itself begin with its own willingness to be tested. The Barmen Declaration of the German Confessing Church of 1934 began in just such a way: "Try the spirits whether they are of God! Prove also the words of the Confessional Synod of the German Evangelical Church to see whether they agree with Holy Scripture and with the Confessions of the Fathers. If you find that we are speaking contrary to Scripture, then do not listen to us! But if you find that we are taking our stand upon Scripture, then let no fear or temptation keep you from treading with us the path of faith and obedience to the Word of God, in order that God's people be of one mind upon earth and that we in faith experience what he himself has said: 'I will never leave you, nor forsake you.' Therefore, 'Fear not, little flock, for it is your Father's good pleasure to give you the kingdom.' "

Christians through the centuries have discovered that such a confidence in the Bible results in our greatest freedom from bondage to the false and the exotic. If we are not clear about this fundamental confidence, we shall be easily victimized throughout our Christian lives by the visions and dreams of people around us. Apart from this standard for testing doctrines we have no defense against their visions—or, for that matter, our own visions. They claim so much and try so hard to convince us that, since the vision or experience is more recent than older truth, it is more relevant. Moreover, they may support the new spiritual breakthrough with dramatic illustrations of power—and we remember from historical experience that public support quickly gathers around any proof of power.

How are we to answer the claims that now become the underpinnings of whole new schemes and elaborate doctrines? I believe that over the long pull the best corrective in the face of error is the positive affirmation of the truth and the demonstration of what Francis Schaeffer calls the "mark of the Christian"—

the love of Christ at work through us toward others. Jesus Christ is the one who finally proves substantial when the exotic movements have crumbled.

The Authority of the Biblical Text

What then constitutes loyalty to the biblical witness in the teaching and preaching mandate of the church? Confusion over this question has been created by the fact that most of the Christian churches and most of the quasi-Christian movements as well claim loyalty to the Bible.

Our search for a clear answer brings us to the important role of biblical and theological study in the life of the Christian and the church. The vigorous practice of theology and biblical exegesis (the accurate rendering of the essential content of a text) is vital for the health of the church in the world today. What does the text say (exegesis)? What does it mean and how does the individual part of the biblical teaching relate and fit together with the whole (biblical theology)? Then finally, what are the overall themes and conclusions that we may draw together in order to form the basis of affirming our faith to the world (systematic theology)?

In each step of the way, the testing process should be encouraged and never discouraged; our work and our conclusions must not be absolutized. The one absolute in Christian faith is God himself and his Speech. Our faith, our affirmations, even our doctrines about the Bible itself are not absolute, nor do our theological conclusions have final binding authority. Every Christian must always put to every doctrine the question, What is the evidence? Not of my feelings, nor of the popular folk preference, nor of the historical appearances around us—but what is the evidence of the biblical texts themselves? There is continuous need for the earnest testing of doctrine. It is particularly important to stay out of that situation in which a congregation or an individual develops preferences for a few approved themes and then honors as "sound" the teaching that emphasizes them while avoiding others. In fact, such teaching may not be biblical at all; it may simply be the confirmation of popular folk theology.

It is not surprising that the work of serious Bible study is not necessarily a popular enterprise. The honest exposition of the text of the Bible is what God's people need, but it is not always what his people desire.

The Authority of Biblical Themes in Our Lives

Biblical authority in the church is a broader question for the pastor than only the determination of the teaching content of biblical texts. The question requires us to consider now this larger landscape: How can I be a biblical Christian in my own style of life, in church government, in pastoral counseling?

The basic principle involved here, it seems to me, is that the biblical Christian is prepared to order faith and life on the basis of the gospel. Biblical Christianity has Jesus Christ as center. What matters here is the daily walk of the Christian man and woman with Christ by faith. Prayer, simple obedience, confession of our sins, and acceptance of our belovedness are the ingredients of the Christian life that the Bible invites us to enter into and enjoy. As a result of the personal relationship with the living Christ and the supportive ministry of the Holy Spirit to us in the life of the people of God, the biblical witness draws us into the mandates of the way of discipleship in the world. When it comes to the content of faith, the question that the biblical Christian submits to is this: "If I can be shown that the Bible teaches a doctrine I will believe it." That is the real issue, not how gloriously a Christian speaks about the Bible. But more to the point than the superlatives used to describe its wonder is simply this: Are we prepared to order the way we live and believe on the basis of the Bible's teaching?

Here we must consider some criteria for the use of Scripture in our relationships within the church. As we test out doctrines with one another, some themes become very clear and definite;

others are less clear and, therefore, we are able to be less definite in our advocacy of them. For some doctrines there is strong textual evidence which encourages us to endorse them boldly, while others with less such evidence should be advocated with more modest restraint. For example, we preach many more sermons about the resurrection of Jesus Christ than about the one-sentence mention of baptism on behalf of the dead (1 Cor. 15:29). The one doctrine—the victory of Christ—has clearly more authority for preaching and, therefore, we commend it heartily to those around us. But the one sentence about a baptism for the dead is too obscure of itself and in its setting for us to develop a strong doctrine. We are not completely certain of what Paul means by his reference to it. Therefore, we dare not urge it upon the brothers and sisters in the church.

The same principles apply to the doctrine concerning the woman's role in the church. In this case there are many different pieces of evidence which do not easily fit together to form one simple doctrinal position. Paul urges women to be silent in church (1 Tim. 2), yet he does not urge silence upon the women who prophesy in 1 Corinthians 11. Where such problems of interpretation occur, either because of a scarcity of textual evidence or because of the presence of many different teachings upon a theme, the biblical Christian must show restraint proportionate to the clarity of the whole biblical portrait. We must learn how to discover the relative biblical weight of a particular theme by relating each doctrinal concept we meet to those greater themes which the Bible floods with evidence and confirmation.

The first great theologian in the pages of the Gospels is John the Baptist. In John 3:22–36 we have an example of his theological method in a dialogue between him and members of the Pharisaic party.[4] Every Christian pastor is frequently drawn into similar encounters in which a distinctive feature or theological emphasis with which we are identified is a point of debate. In this discussion about baptisms and rites of purification John the Baptist proves to be as wise a theologian as he is daring a prophet. He seeks for the larger context within which the smaller theme of "baptism and rites of purification" may be helpfully considered. It is clear from the dialogue recorded for us that John the Baptist realizes what the real question is: the mighty act of God himself in Jesus Christ to which every other theme must receive its own true meaning and weight.

A conversation with my children a few days ago illustrates the point. Our ten-year-old son, Jon, asked the question: "Dad, how does a cassette recorder work?" Our daughter Elizabeth, age six, quickly jumped in to answer, "You press this button on the top." Jon seemed unimpressed, so she tried again: "Look Jon, these two wheels turn like this." Jon still declined her answer: "No, I know all that." She still had answers: "Maybe you didn't push the right button." His patience was wearing thin because it finally became clear that what he wanted was not the information about which switches to turn but the answer to a deeper question—how the music of John Denver is electronically impressed upon the tape. At this point it was Elizabeth who began to lose interest. Anne, our ninth-grader, was better able to carry on the conversation Jon had in mind.

The biblical Christian as theologian must continually move with each question toward the deeper, larger themes. For this task we need each other—those who understand our questions and those who misunderstand. John the Baptist needed the intense questions of the Pharisees to help him clarify and understand the larger issues beyond the practices of first-century baptisms. In the same way, we in our century are aided in our own theological clarification by the challenges that come to us from the world around us. Speaking of his antagonist John Eck, Martin Luther said: "So, too, Eck provoked me. He made me wide awake. . . . Accordingly our opponents are very useful to us, although they think they do us harm." [5]

But of even more importance to us in the task of understanding the meaning of doctrines is the twofold humility that should characterize every biblical Christian: first, our prayer to the Lord to be our leader in understanding the intent of Scripture;

and second, the check-and-balance help of our brothers and sisters in Christ—the church. This is the importance of the historic confessions of the church: they give guidance. So also our relationship with the contemporary church gives guidance in helping us to understand what the Scriptures teach.

Martin Luther offered two rules that he followed in interpreting Holy Scripture: "First, if some passage is obscure I consider whether it treats of grace or of law, whether wrath or the forgiveness of sin [is contained in it] and with which of these it agrees better. By this procedure I have often understood the most obscure passages. . . . The second rule is that if the meaning is ambiguous I ask those who have a better knowledge of the language than I have whether the Hebrew/Greek words can bear this or that sense . . . and that is most fitting which is closest to the argument of the book." [6]

Luther's two rules are essential. First, he looks for the larger context within which the particular teaching belongs. Second, he always works hard really to understand meanings of the words in their own language and usage, and what the text means when understood within its own textual setting.

The biblical Christian cares about the teaching of the text itself and endeavors to build from the text to the theme. In my view this is why biblical theology as a discipline should always precede systematic theology. This is how the best doctrines are developed, and the best sermons too. Out of serious Bible study comes the most relevant thematic teaching.

Rules for Biblical Interpretation

Let us move beyond Luther's advice concerning obscure texts and see interpretation in its larger task.

What then are the rules for the interpretation of a biblical text? Our task as preachers/teachers is not simply to read the Bible aloud, but to say in our own words what we think and feel it means. At this point we need guidelines and criteria. Think of some of the steps involved in interpretation:

1. The first is to *establish the text*. The tools for this work are universally available and applicable. Fortunately for the English-speaking Bible interpreter, we have an extensive and very rich resource in the many English translations of the Bible available today. Each of these represents the work of scholars in endeavoring to establish the best English reading of the Greek/Hebrew text, in the same way Luther worked to produce a German text. Though few of us as pastors will become involved in actual translation, yet we also must begin the interpretive journey with literary analysis that seeks out the linguistic meaning of the sentences and of the words used.

2. The second step in interpretation is to determine the meaning and purpose of the text within its own biblical setting. What does the text mean? At this step our own value judgments come into play; the soundest interpretations come from moving slowly and carefully to learn from the whole context of the whole passage or book what the writer is saying. The general rule is that the meaning of each separate part is principally governed by the meaning of the larger part. For example, to find the meaning of one sentence of Paul we must first look to that sentence's larger paragraph; then to the collections of paragraphs, then to the book, and finally to the total body of Pauline literature.

3. A further step in the interpretive journey concerns the meaning of the text within its own early church setting. A New Testament passage might require us to ask such a question as: What is the situation within the church which receives or writes a document? For example, what were the problems in Corinth to which Paul was speaking in his Corinthian letters? In an Old Testament study we might ask what purpose in temple worship a psalm might serve. Such background questions are not only of great interpretive help but lead us to study the cultural-historical-religious setting of New Testament and Old Testament eras.

4. The final step in interpretation is to draw up theological conclusions and imperatives, pastoral encouragement and

prophetic exhortation, which are then affirmed to the people. We call all of this a sermon.

But often the interpreter's pilgrimage from the text read to the meaning proclaimed is roadblocked by lack of hard work, by preconceived theological agendas, or by careless methods of workmanship. I won't make accusations on the hard work question, but the latter two causes of roadblocks deserve some attention.

Somewhere within the interpreter's journey from text to theology, hidden agendas and careless methods have sometimes conspired to produce very shaky biblical teaching. An example of this is what happened to New Testament form criticism in our own century. Form criticism strongly emphasized the importance of the historical-theological forces at work within the early church itself. The form critics reasoned that since the New Testament documents were written by the primitive church, the most crucial clue to the correct interpretation of any passage was the right understanding of the motives at work within the early church. But this method of analysis often tended to become so absorbed in its search for those motives that it would not allow a narrative in the Gospels to speak simply and directly in its own terms. Reading the Gospel accounts through this grid system tended to result in the double guessing of each passage. Thus the actual literary context of the biblical material was often disregarded in favor of the interpreter's theory as to how a New Testament incident might have been written and/or created by an early church writer in order to support some doctrine important to him. Checked and balanced by historical research and respect for the biblical text itself, this form critical method is very useful, but without those restraints there develops an interpretive arrogance which grants to itself too much certainty.

British New Testament scholar T. W. Manson wrote: "To speak candidly, I find myself, after a good deal of labour in this field, being gradually driven to the conclusion that much that passes for historical study of the life of Jesus consists not in asking of any story in the tradition: 'is it credible in itself?' but: 'what motive could the church have had for telling this tale?' which can easily become the question: 'what motives led the church to invent it?' The danger is that what is entitled 'Life of Jesus' or the like should turn out to be in fact a psychological novel about a large number of anonymous members of the primitive church." [7]

I believe that the greatest dangers to biblical interpretation today are the various grid systems we superimpose upon the text ahead of time and through which we then demand that the text be read.

Protestant liberals of the nineteenth and twentieth centuries placed just that sort of interpretive grid upon the Bible in order to find in the Bible what they were looking for. They wanted a life of Jesus without miracles, eschatology, or heavy teaching on the tragedy of humanity. They wanted ethical encouragement with a safe amount of divine endorsement. Their methodology, therefore, searched for a "historical" Jesus minus the features that nineteenth-century idealism found embarrassing. Form criticism enabled them to give to the early church responsibility for the "not approved" theological themes that are in the Bible, and to keep for their Jesus those parts which contained the approved themes. [8]

In 1941 Rudolph Bultmann reversed form criticism's theological preferences. He found that, instead of rejecting the early church's Easter faith, it was that very eschatological faith which we in our century should embrace. The tragedy in his form-critical methodology is that Jesus still remains the variable while it is the Easter faith of the primitive church that becomes the new constant.

Ernst Käsemann commented: "Bultmann expressly adopts as his own H. Braun's statement 'The constant is the self-understanding of the believers; Christology is the variable.' I hold this judgment to be, quite simply, false, and to pick up Bultmann's own distinction, false both historically and materially." [9]

There are other grid systems which also superimpose upon

the biblical texts theological decisions that cannot be found within the text itself. The C. I. Scofield notes and textual paragraph titles found in the Scofield Bible for Matthew 5, 6, 7 and Revelation 3 are examples of texts that are squeezed into a previously made context which the interpreter brought to the text ahead of time.

Fortunately, there is a rule of thumb that will protect both the text from distortion and the interpreter from speculative error. Insisting upon the primacy of the literary analysis of the text itself will permit a biblical text the right first of all to speak in its own terms.

Developing a Biblical Ministry

How does a pastor express and develop a biblical ministry in the church today? I believe this begins with one's own self-awareness, one's own theological decision to be a biblical Christian in the first place.

It also requires *work* that must be done and skills that must be learned. Serious biblical preaching and teaching and small group Bible study in the context of a local congregation or gathering of Christians are important ways in which a pastor may fulfill the mandate to build up the body of Christ.

In the matter of our self-awareness and the role of our own individual priority decisions, let me comment that one of the very great privileges and dilemmas of the professional ministry is the *right to time* granted to the pastor by the congregation in its care and support of him. This right to time means that the pastor has to a very large degree, varying from situation to situation, the authority to arrange and organize each week. For many in the clergy this authority is carelessly squandered through poor planning, but for others it becomes a creative means of exercising the stewardship of freedom—an opportunity that few professions experience to the same degree. Add to this the tradition of most churches which insures a free pulpit, and we can appreciate the immense freedom that we who are ordinary Christian pastors have in which to express concretely whatever are the convictions and goals of our lives. We choose the subject matter for seminars we may offer and the texts for sermons. The words and attitudes to be expressed in counseling are ours. We decide on the goals for study, and within the limits of our budget we select the books in our library.

As I reflect upon my own ministry, I realize that small Bible study and biblical theological study groups played a key role in my own student days both in Berkeley and at Princeton Seminary. The Bible study group at Barrington Hall at the University of California had first challenged me to think through the claims of Christianity from a "no-holds-barred" adult perspective. Then at Princeton I became involved in numerous small Bible study groups with Princeton University students. These one-hour-per-week discussion groups were very formative in my life, both spiritually and theologically. They were a proving ground for young theologians in the making. The groups were robust and critical in the best sense, so that every Christian theme was always under scrutiny and evaluation. The groups welcomed non-Christians, and when several of these became Christians, each of us saw in a practical, down-to-earth way that the Holy Spirit confirms the words of a New Testament book to the life of a student.

Our task as believers in a Bible study group was simply to do our best honestly to understand what the text was saying. We also learned in that atmosphere that Christians do not always come to identical conclusions given the same evidence. There are some who observe that pastors who only preach may not make that discovery. When I graduated from seminary and began my own career as minister to students at University Presbyterian Church in Seattle, small Bible study groups were a major part of my own teaching/growing strategy—at church, in homes, on campus, among men, among women, with highschoolers, collegians, adults—and I found that the pastor grows as well as teaches. I am personally indebted to countless seminars and discussions for the theological breakthroughs in understanding a text that have often played a key role in my own theological integration. As a pastor I was of course permitted the privilege of public preaching and teaching, and I made the choice early in my own career to concentrate primarily upon a teaching style of preaching. This has lent itself to serious biblical and theological preaching where people in the congregation are invited also to consider the theme or book on their own along with the preacher.

My second ministry was as pastor at Union Church of Manila in the Philippines. The question in that new setting was, Would adults who are busy and from many different church and national cultural backgrounds also be interested in serious Bible and theological study? I found that they were as eager for serious study as were students. A weekly adult Bible class and small early morning study groups were organized there. I found the key in small groups to be a personal invitation to the potential participants and an inductive study format [10] that enabled each member to feel the value of his own input. At Manila I saw many adults and youth become excited about the Christian faith, and the same has been true in Berkeley; lay people want to study along with the pastor.

When we reflect upon the goals and strategies that express themselves in the use of time, in the themes and kinds of preaching, in the format of small groups, in the method of personal research and study, we see revealed the basic inner decision of the individual pastor. Each of us as minister shows the priorities that are motivationally most important to us by the way we spend the week.

Preparing for Biblical Preaching

"The tediousness of Christian preaching is undoubtedly a greater danger to the church than all historical criticism put together." [11] This statement by Ernst Käsemann shows one New Testament scholar's estimate of the importance of preaching for the life of the church. But to express in preaching a biblical ministry that is not simply tedious requires much of the pastor. Let me focus upon four areas that deserve priority from all of us: (1) the work of research into the text; (2) the work of developing a theological perspective; (3) the work of pastoral sensitivity and prophetic listening; (4) the work of message preparation and communication.

1. Is it not possible to argue that too much study is dangerous? Perhaps a pastor would do best to shun all research into the Bible and instead major in a simple daily walk with Christ and a ministry that cares about people and seeks to help them with their pressing human needs. Might not such priorities greatly upset the weekly study schedule of the pastor? I bring this up just as we are to consider the research mandate for a pastor in order to make the point that even so important a task as the calling seriously to study the gospel is itself subject to the greater mandate to obey the gospel. Obedience to Christ may very well shatter the well-organized week and bring a minister to Sunday morning intellectually unprepared for the task of biblical preaching. On such an occasion I believe the pastor should pray for the help of the Lord. But I think it is a fair observation to make about pastors in general that the better organized the week the better able we are to take on the heavy demands of human need for which no one can plan ahead. Also, the prayer for help when I am unprepared and when I threw away the chances I had to be prepared should not be called faith—it is impudence. The fact is this: there is historical content to the gospel, and that historical content deserves our hard work and study in order that its message may become clear.

The ordinary preaching/teaching pastor should go about the research task in the Old Testament/New Testament documents with the same earnestness that a scientist uses in working with the basic data of his or her particular discipline. Blocks of time must be set apart for foundation-building study in the Bible itself and in other support tools to Bible study. Lexical study of Greek and Hebrew is a prerequisite to making full use of serious commentaries and doing the word studies which are at the core of all exegesis. Since in serious Bible study the pastor is in effect writing a commentary in brief upon each passage that will later appear as the basis for preaching, he needs some workable system of preserving the results, book by book, of the work already done.

The value of a commentary methodology in Bible study is that at its center is the art of posing questions to the text, a skill of very great usefulness, since the heart of communication consists in addressing meaningful questions that are in the minds of the listener.

2. The next stage in research is the development of a theological perspective, that is, the pastor's own conclusion as to what is the main burden of the text. The commentary method naturally leads here, as the teaching of a text is understood in its own context and related to other biblical themes, then finally related to contemporary questions and issues of the first century and of our own generation.

3. The pastor who is a good listener to people and a thoughtful observer of culture is better able to build bridges between the historical Good News and the contemporary setting in which we live today. A very large part of communication originates in the accuracy with which we have been able to feel and understand the real feelings and expectations of people. Prophetic listening has a very deep spiritual dimension about it too. It means being attentive to people, and most of all attentive to God. I am convinced that a sense of what is called the *burden of the Lord* in the Old Testament prophets is at the heart of the communication of biblical Christianity to a congregation. It is not a pose or a skill but an outgrowth of the way of discipleship, a mixture of the statesmanship by which the prophet correctly observed the situation with the knowledge of the Word of the Lord, and the love in his heart for the Lord and the people.

4. Preaching may be verbal, but message preparation is primarily a written skill and involves a lot of hard work. Each

minister develops a unique style in the creation of the sermon. As I see it, the principal art involved is that of skillfully narrowing down the very many possible themes in a text to those few most vivid ones, and then properly setting up each theme so than a listener is able to see the point of the text, and to understand what it means for life today.

Timeless Truth for Contemporary Christians

Biblical Christians are not bibliolaters. We worship Jesus Christ, not the Holy Bible. The Bible, taken seriously, never stimulates false worship, but by its texts and themes, its history and poetry, its yearnings and prayers, its real people from Moses to John, points us to its Lord. Therefore, when the Bible is truly authoritative for our faith, there is little danger of that faith becoming sidetracked with insignificant themes and cultic curiosities.

Because of the timelessness of Jesus Christ himself, the Bible's witness to his ministry is also timeless. The biblical Christian is not in bondage to the tyranny of the current, to the oppressive pressure of the "in" cause. The James party at Galatia must have panicked many Greek Christians with the "new word" that the truest Christians would not only believe in Christ but also become Jewish. But Paul had the larger context of the gospel to apply to their claims and, out of that controversy, the Book of Galatians became a declaration of independence for all Christians who have ever been browbeaten by the latest fad or movement. The biblical Christian is free from false gods because the Bible has bound us to the true God.

Biblical faith does not blunt one's ability to be a shrewd observer of the contemporary scene. I believe the pressure of the gospel rather creates just the opposite result—a sharpened sensitivity and inquisitiveness growing out of a stance toward life that does not need to fear truth wherever one finds it. The Bible has committed us to the way of truth without equivocation. "Walk in the light as he [God] is in the light" (1 John 7).

And yet this inquisitiveness is not a form of irresponsibility toward life. There is a doctrinal wanderlust that often takes hold of a person. It tends to create its own momentum, and within it an insatiable appetite for the new and different for their own sake.

This wanderlust should not be confused with the research instinct that we have been describing, or the hard work of theological inquiry. The restlessness in research is founded upon the whole principle of testing followed by meaningful response to truth discovered, whereas the restlessness of doctrinal wanderlust is dominated by inner moods, by the current immediate impression. Wanderlust is not freedom, though it disguises itself as freedom. In the classic river scene in *Huckleberry Finn* it is the slave, Jim, who is in the truest sense free—not Huck—because Jim knows who he is, whereas Huck at that point in the story is simply a young boy adrift on the Mississippi.

I can think of no more exciting task in our age, so often adrift, and yet underneath it all so hungry for the real, than to have the privilege of sharing in the witness to Jesus Christ, the same yesterday, today and tomorrow.

THE CURRENT TENSIONS:
IS THERE A WAY OUT?

by David Hubbard

David Allan Hubbard is President and Professor of Old Testament, Fuller Theological Seminary, Pasadena, California. He is also Executive Vice-President of Fuller Evangelistic Association and speaker for the international radio broadcast "The Joyful Sound." He is President of the Association of Theological Schools in the United States and Canada, a member of the board of directors of the National Institute of Campus Ministries, and recently completed a 3-year term as member of the California State Board of Education. In addition to having written more than twenty books, Dr. Hubbard has contributed to a number of major works (Baker's Dictionary of Theology, The New Bible Dictionary, The Biblical Expositor, The Wycliffe Commentary, the Higley Commentary, The KJV Holman Family Bible); *and his articles have frequently appeared in such magazines as* Christianity Today, Eternity, The Christian Herald *and* World Vision, *among others. Together with Bernard Ramm, Vernon Grounds, and Billy Graham, he contributed to the symposium* Is God Dead? *Dr. Hubbard holds the B.A. from Westmont College (Santa Barbara, California), the B.D. and Th.M. from Fuller Theological Seminary, and the Ph.D. in Old Testament and Semitics from St. Andrews University in Scotland. In 1975 he was awarded the D.D. by John Brown University and the L.H.D. by Rockford College. Dr. Hubbard is a member of the American Academy of Religion and the Society of Biblical Literature and Exegesis, and is listed in Who's Who in America.*

How CAN WE LET the Bible be what it is? That is the question at stake in the current debate among evangelicals. From biblical days until now, the people of God have treasured God's Word as his authoritative guide to what they believed and how they lived. The power of that Word in the oracles of the prophets and the preaching of the apostles has transformed their lives by confronting them with the judgment and grace of the living God.

Our experience of the Word has brought both blessing and tension. The blessing has come from knowing that God has spoken and acted to make himself known and to reconcile us to himself. The tension has come as we have sought the best ways to honor God's truth and protect it against the attacks of unbelievers.

This is no new problem. It has faced the people of God in many forms through the past twenty centuries. In the days of Jesus the debate centered in the issue of the Old Testament's purpose. Was it law to regulate the lives of God's people in their religious conduct and moral decision, as the Pharisees claimed? They sought to honor God by clinging to and amplifying the laws given in their Torah. Without invalidating the law, Jesus went on to teach the prophetic and messianic purposes of the Scriptures which prepared for his life-giving mission. One of his aims was to help us see that God's Word was more than a handbook of religious devotion; it was a declaration of hope in the salvation God would bring.

Again, in the early centuries, the church wrestled with the message of the Old Testament. One wing of the church, centered chiefly in Alexandria, Egypt, had great difficulty with the stern law, the harsh judgments, the strange morals, and the human ways of speaking of God—his hands, feet, eyes—that the Old Testament contained. They felt that for those sections to be the Word of God there must be found in them deep, hidden, allegorical meanings about spiritual realities, moral teachings, or heavenly promises. Another wing, based in Antioch, Syria, sought to interpret the Bible literally wherever possible and used the allegorical method only sparingly.

At the Reformation, the question of how best to honor the Bible focused on the clarity and sufficiency and authority of the Bible. Could believers understand it and interpret it without the help of church officials? Did it by itself say all that we need to know about God and his way of salvation? Or, as the Roman Catholic church had contended, were the traditions and interpretations of the church also necessary to complete our religious knowledge? Protestant reformers rightly answered those questions with the words *sola scriptura*—Scripture alone. Scripture by itself is clear, sufficient, and authoritative in bringing to us the news of God's salvation and the way in which that salvation changes human conduct and human destiny. Catholic theologians and ecclesiastics at the Council of Trent (1545-1563) said no. For them, God's pattern of revelation was not *sola scriptura* but *ecclesia et scriptura:* the church, teaching, interpreting, and augmenting Scripture with tradition. The Reformers had fought for a truth, the full implications of which we still need to reckon with: When God speaks what further proof do we need of his authority? Does the living God need human validation of the authority of his Word?

During the nineteenth century, under the impetus of higher critical studies and humanistic philosophy, the problem of honoring the Scripture took another turn: Was the Bible another ancient, oriental book, whose sources, backgrounds, and themes were to be studied without any commitment to the belief that God was speaking in the Scriptures? A whole army of scholars in Europe and the New World seemed to go at their tasks as though that were the case. And to combat that line of thought, God-fearing teachers and scholars fervently sought to resist the onslaughts of that skeptical higher criticism and to honor the Bible as God's authoritative and inspired Word.

At stake in each of these eras—from apostolic days until our own century—is the nature of the Bible. What does it mean for it to be the Word of God? How do we read the Bible so as truly to hear God's Word through it? How do we defend the authority and truthfulness of God's Word against those who would malign them?

The temptation that devout churchmen have often faced is to overreact to the assaults against the Bible. As their opponents distort the message or undercut the authority of Scripture, the protectors of orthodoxy may be tempted to defend the Bible in a way that muffles its message or obscures its purpose. If many Jews treasured the laws of God unduly, some early Christians made the mistake of acting as though their faith in Christ freed them from all obligation to lead moral lives. When Marcion and his followers rejected the Old Testament as an unworthy book with a false picture of God, their opponents like Origen chose to rescue the Old Testament from their attacks by imposing on it a method of interpretation foreign to it—an allegorical interpretation in which each passage was thought to contain several levels of truth: spiritual, moral, and eschatological. Their motive was right: the Old Testament cannot be set aside in any Christian view of Scripture. Their method was wrong, setting a pattern of interpretation that made it hard for the church to hear the true message of the Old Testament until the Reformation was almost at hand.[1]

In the seventeenth century, the adversaries of Protestant orthodoxy influenced the disciples of Luther and Calvin to develop theories of inspiration more meticulous than any the church had yet seen. The Socinians, based in Poland, used arguments grounded in human reason to attack biblical doctrines like the Trinity and the resurrection of all men. Their Reformed opponents resorted to extreme rationalistic attempts to defend the Bible's full authority by claiming that even the Hebrew vowel-points were inspired, not realizing that the vowels in the Old Testament text were not present in the original manuscripts but were added almost a thousand years after the Old Testament was completed. Faced by the Socinians, by the Catholic Counter Reformation with its commitment to tradition and Scripture as the twin pillars of spiritual authority, and by the changes brought to the view of science by Copernicus, Lutherans like Johann Gerhard (1582–1637) and Abraham Calovius (1612–1686) developed arguments for the inspiration of Scripture that put so much stress on Scripture's divine origin that they came close to obscuring the human contribution. The Reformed emphasis on the saving message of Scripture was shifted somewhat to put more stress on the words and phrases of Scripture itself. For the first time, theological arguments began to focus on the inerrancy of Scripture as well as on its sufficiency and clarity. One of the ways in which the seventeenth-century theologians defended the plenary inspiration of Scripture was to insist that if the inspiration of any part of the Bible were in doubt, the inspiration of the whole would be put in question. This "all or nothing" approach to biblical authority has considerable bearing on the present debate. In the Calvinist wing of the church, Francis Turretin took a similar approach. His influence, which reaches to the present evangelical discussion, is sketched in Jack Rogers's essay in this volume.

The nineteenth century saw history virtually repeat itself. The issues were similar, but the cast had changed. This time one chief adversary was Friedrich D. E. Schleiermacher (1768–1834), probably Protestantism's most influential theologian in the centuries between John Calvin and Karl Barth. Schleiermacher, reacting against the rationalism of the seventeenth-

century Lutherans, was selective in his use of the Old
Testament, to which he ascribed only a little more worth than
he did to Greek philosophy—both being part of the preparation
for Christianity. He was also high-handed in his treatment of
the Christological passages of the New Testament, which he
reinterpreted as evidence for his view that Jesus was a man who
perfectly exemplified that dependence on God which for Schleiermacher was the essence of true religion.

During the same period, a rationalistic approach to the Scriptures was developing, especially in Germany, which showed
great suspicion toward the biblical miracles and other events
that witness to supernatural intervention. The pinnacle of this
approach was the publication of Julius Wellhausen's *Prolego-
mena to the History of Israel* (1878). Applying evolutionary
principles learned from both Charles Darwin and G. W. F.
Hegel, Wellhausen radically restructured the Old Testament by
attempting to demonstrate a naturalistic development of Israel's
faith and to rearrange the order of Old Testament narratives so
that substantial parts of the Pentateuch were held to have origi-
nated not in the time of Moses but as late as the time of Ezra.

The names of Schleiermacher and Wellhausen can serve as
shorthand for the dramatic changes which challenged many
scholars of the church in regard to their attitudes toward the
inspiration and authority of the Bible. Understandably threatened by these assaults and by the rise of Unitarianism in New
England, American evangelicals sought to stem the erosion of
confidence in the Bible by defining more precisely than had
the Reformers the nature of inspiration and authority. Expectedly, they turned for help to Turretin, who had developed a
case for the divinity of Scripture based on rationalistic arguments about the nature of inspiration and what it implies. None
did this with more persistence nor effectiveness than the Princeton stalwarts Charles Hodge (1797–1878) and Benjamin Breck-
inridge Warfield (1851–1921).

Since the methods of their defense have been sketched by
Jack Rogers, we need to note here only their tendency to fight

the rationalism of their opponents with a counterrationalism that protected the Scripture in the following ways: (1) they inferred from their doctrine of inspiration an inerrancy that extended to every detail of every kind of statement of Scripture; (2) they argued not for the inerrancy of any present texts of Scripture but of the original autographs to which no generation of the church has ever had access; (3) as both apologists and theologians they sought to protect the Scripture against all attack so as to gain the right to use all of Scripture as the groundwork of their theology, but in so doing they often gave their followers the impression that no part of Scripture could be believed and trusted unless all parts of it could be proved to be inerrant. A consequence of their strategy was to shift many American evangelicals away from the Reformed emphasis on the majesty of biblical doctrine and the inner witness of the Spirit as the chief evidences of the Bible's inspiration and authority. Their strategy has led also, in much of conservative biblical scholarship, to a defensiveness that finds it necessary to try to harmonize all biblical statements with each other and with the results of scientific and archeological discovery. At times the effect of the work of Hodge and Warfield has been to divert the church's attention from the central themes of Scripture and its saving message to the details of science, history, and geography which are touched on in its pages.[2]

This brief sketch of some of the church's tensions in regard to the interpretation and inspiration of the Bible has one purpose: to show how orthodox attempts to react to heresy or unbelief, necessary as they are, often bring overreactions. In the long centuries of church history, one extreme has frequently provoked another.

Dealing with the Bible is not unlike the basic rule of golf: we must play the ball where it lies. We must not let either friends or enemies of the faith force us to use strategies of defense or interpretation that do not reckon with the reality of the Bible itself.

How We Got Where We Are—The Liberal-Fundamentalist
Controversy

Standing on this side of the liberal-fundamentalist controversy, we may find it helpful to weigh its results. The smoke of that particular battle, which waged hot and heavy for nearly fifty years, started to thin out after World War II, when the breezes of the neo-orthodox theologies of Barth, Brunner, and Bonhoeffer began to blow on our shores. The battle itself has abated somewhat—in the sense that the old optimistic, humanistic liberalism has been replaced with a deeper understanding of human sin, divine grace, biblical revelation, and Christian discipleship. But the effects of that battle are much with us and cry out for clarification.

The defense of the Bible's authority which Hodge, Warfield, and the Princeton school set up has kept sound *the confidence in the Scriptures* of literally millions of Christian people. Our debt to them is substantial.

At the same time it is only fair to mention that one of the side results has been a *misunderstanding of the place of biblical scholarship*. It is not that the Princeton school was directly responsible for this. Indeed, men like Warfield, Robert Dick Wilson, and J. Grescham Machen were models of scholarly ardor and discipline. Yet often, to the minds of conservative evangelicals, because of the particular situation in which Hodge and Warfield worked, the scholars became the enemy. After all, it was scholars who had questioned the accuracy and validity of the Bible in the first place. The label "higher critic" became a largely negative term to describe the skeptically minded professors who picked and probed at the biblical documents, trying to prove that they were not what the church through the ages had claimed them to be.[3] And many biblical scholars had justly earned that reputation.

But the task of scholarship remains essential even though it is sometimes done badly or put to destructive purposes. The answer to skeptical, negative study of the Bible is not to ban investigation, but to engage in better investigation. The full meaning of the Bible—despite the basic clarity of the Bible's message of salvation, taught by the Reformers and confirmed in our experience—cannot be discerned apart from sincere, thorough, and devout investigation of (1) the meaning of biblical language, (2) the background—historical, cultural, political— of the biblical events, (3) the types of literature through which God has spoken, (4) the situations in the life of Israel or the church which sparked comment from prophet or apostle, and (5) the process by which the Spirit of God produced the books which he has caused his people to gather in the Bible.

Another legacy of the nineteenth-century evangelical scholars, whose heirs we are, is the *strong system of apologetics* with which they defended the faith. In an era when the church was confronted with many reasons why the historic doctrines should not be believed, evangelicals were offered a solid basis on which to ground their beliefs. The rationalistic attacks on the validity of God's Word and the reality of divine revelation were met by what were considered iron-clad arguments that proved the entire Bible to be the Word of God, and, if the Word of God, then inerrant in all its teachings and details. Who knows how many thousands of intelligent Christians were armed to maintain their system of belief by these apologetic tools?

But the legacy—precious though it be—has not been without defects. Where it is proposed that the divine character of Scripture is established by the inerrancy of even the minutest detail and that this in turn must become an essential item of faith, any negative evidence from scholarly investigation—whether scientific, historical, archeological, or literary—has the possibility of placing faith itself in jeopardy. If the strong reasonings of Warfield and his followers have "saved the faith" of some believers, they may also have "cost the faith" of others. Faced with the conflict between a doctrine of "literal" inerrancy and the conclusions of respected biblical scholars that seemed to contradict it, they felt forced either to give up their system of belief or to give up their sense of intellectual integrity. Where literal inerrancy is made the chief defense of the truth of the gospel, a collapse of belief in that definition of inerrancy may lead to a collapse of trust in the gospel itself. Does not the statement of a prime reviewer of Harold Lindsell's *The Battle for the Bible* imply this? "[Abandoning inerrancy] raises an unanswerable question regarding the determination of accuracy in the Bible and also effectively undermines its reliability." [4] Articles in a creed tend to stand and fall together. Where inerrancy becomes a creedal issue—which it never did for the Reformers—the other items in that creed may be victims of doubt when inerrancy is called into question.[5]

The worthy, even crucial, *emphasis on the inspiration of all parts* of the Bible has made an invaluable contribution to the health and power of the evangelical movement. It has helped us resist the error, so typical of theological liberalism, of treating some parts of Scripture as divine word while ignoring or even rejecting others. It has caused us to treasure all parts of Scripture and to seek to apply their teachings to our life and thought. It has encouraged devotional reading and Bible study in millions of homes and thousands of churches. Bible schools and Bible conferences have sprung up in every region of the land to give opportunity for a closer acquaintance with God's Word.

Yet even this contribution has been a blessing somewhat mixed. The emphasis on the inspiration of all parts of the Bible has sometimes resulted in *the attempt to apply equally all parts of the Bible to our conduct and doctrine.* Promises given specifically to one person in a special context have been appropriated by believers in ways that have no warrant. Texts from Zophar or Bildad have been claimed as life-verses, without any appreciation of the role in revelation that those "friends" of Job were called to play. The close-your-eyes-and-point-to-a-verse form of determining God's will is only a slight caricature of the way well-meaning people have used the Bible.

In our zeal to seek spiritual truth from even the most minute parts of the Scripture we have frequently been led to neglect the major theological themes that are its heart—the revelation of

God's glory and grace in the face of human sin and the sending of the Christ to reveal God's nature and reconcile us to God's favor. Detailed study of the parts is essential. But it has often kept us so close to God's canvas that we have failed to stand back and let the whole painting speak to us of God's grand design for our salvation.

While we have rightly treasured every book, every verse, every line, every word of the sixty-six sacred documents, we have not always been eager to hear what those words mean. Sometimes it is our very doctrine of literalistic inerrancy that has gotten in our way. If every verse is equally God's Word, then may we not look for a special, even hidden, meaning in every verse? Unhappily allegorical interpretation which the Reformers wisely left behind them has often been brought back into our biblical exposition as part of our attempt to defend the spirituality of the entire text. One has only to cite the common evangelical interpretations of the wilderness tabernacle or Solomon's Song to make the point.

The wrong definition of inerrancy has often led to the opposite extreme from allegory—a literalism that fails to understand how biblical truth comes to us in literary forms. Modern standards of accuracy have been imposed on books that God was pleased to inspire in ancient Oriental contexts, with their very different standards of accuracy. Claims have been made about the meaning of the text without recourse to the ancient documents of Egypt, Mesopotamia, and Ugarit which provide part of the background for understanding both the Bible's meaning and its uniqueness. This may have been excusable a hundred years ago at the beginnings of archeological and epigraphical research; it certainly is not in the last quarter of our century.

To revere the Word is admirable; it is, however, no substitute for using every possible—every God-given means—for understanding it. Reading literal meanings where they were not intended or spiritual meanings where they are not present or forcing harmonizations where they were not intended is just as dishonoring to the Bible as failing to hear its intended spiritual message.

The human process by which God chose to make his Word known in earthly languages is as crucial to our knowledge of what he is saying in Scripture as is our recognition of Scripture's full inspiration. The God who chose to speak to us through writers who lived in specific historical, social, cultural, and linguistic contexts has, by that method of speaking, determined how his Word is to be studied. Technical biblical scholarship, when it works correctly, is not a method imposed on Scripture from without. It is an approach demanded from within. In Genesis, God revealed the creation story over against a setting alive with belief in pagan deities and flooded by myths that described the beginnings of human life and history. How can we possibly catch the full thrust of those magnificent early chapters of our Bible if we do not see it against the Middle-Eastern social and religious setting which serves as their backdrop? [6] The Genesis accounts of creation are not at all an academic account of our beginnings. They are a powerful sermon (almost a song) that celebrates God's power and glory over all the elements and objects of the universe which Israel's neighbors falsely worshiped.

Large sections of the Old Testament are written in poetry. They are not to be read as prose; that is obvious. What is not so obvious is that they are written in Hebrew poetry, which means that they have to be interpreted accordingly. The parallelism, the creative repetition which is the heart of Hebrew poetry, has to be considered. So does the nature of Hebrew song, which usually arises out of specific use in daily life. Work songs, love songs, battle songs, worship songs, complaint songs, lament songs, combine with judgment speeches, salvation speeches, court arguments, and a host of other literary forms to comprise what we call Hebrew poetry (and there are at least a similar number of prose forms). A knowledge of Shakespeare or Tennyson helps only a little in reading this kind of poetry. We do best when, by careful investigation of the parallel passages in the Bible and by judicious comparison of the Hebrew literature with its counterparts in other cultures, we don the sandals of those ancients whom God elected as the bearers of his Word.

At no time did God snatch the biblical authors from their settings; at no time did he transform them into other than what they were—citizens of an ancient time and place. Yet it is the wonder of his providence, the miracle of his power, that what they said and how they said it were precisely what he wanted.

Though the examples used are drawn from the Old Testament, the task of accurately reading the New Testament is just as formidable. Take the Gospels, for instance. They represent a unique literary genre, unparalleled anywhere in antiquity. Though the closest parallel may be a book like Jeremiah that both traces a prophet's life and preserves his teachings, we have nowhere in the biblical period a set of writings comparable in style and character to Matthew, Mark, and Luke. This means that we have no clues from outside the Scripture to help us know how to read them. Patience and humility, therefore, have to be the rule, along with a certain amount of trial and error. What is certain is that we must not be content to read Mark as we do the *Los Angeles Times*. Mark has to be understood on his own terms, not on terms which we sons and daughters of a modern Western era bring with us. Indeed, even the *Los Angeles Times* requires considerable hermeneutical insight: we do not read Ann Landers with the same approach we bring to Peanuts; an Associated Press dispatch is different from a letter to the editor, and both are different from the weather predictions, the crossword puzzle, and the used-car ads.

It is basic to our understanding of truth that the literary form and the subject matter contain the keys to their own interpretation. A valentine cries out to be read one way and a recipe another. To confuse them is both to ruffle the course of true love and to jeopardize the workings of our digestive systems.

Hodge and Warfield were able theologians. Unhappily, their theological heirs have not always been. The positive influence of a concern for Bible study which American evangelicals have exhibited has not always been accompanied by an acquaintance with the great theological affirmations of the first four centuries and the Reformation. We have often gone at Christian truth piecemeal. We see that, for example, in a preoccupation with the detailed interpretations of passages in Daniel or Revelation that speak of end-time events. I grew up with a detailed understanding of the precise sequence of events of the end times yet without really knowing why Christ was to come again, what were the purposes of final judgment, what God was seeking to achieve by the resurrection of the dead. I suspect that I was all too typical of many evangelicals formed in a dispensational mold. Forty years later, are we in danger of breeding a generation of evangelicals who have pat answers to the problem passages of biblical prophecy furnished by highly successful best-selling books but who cannot fit the end-time events into the redemptive and creative programs of the triune God?

Adherence to the truth of Scripture without a knowledge of how the best spirits in the church have understood it through the centuries has left many evangelicals ripe for faddistic attractions from Jehovah's Witnesses to British Israel, from Flat Earth societies to outer space cults, from political right-wingism to revolutionary ideologies. If we cut ourselves off, as we sometimes have, from communion with the brightest of the teaching doctors and the soundest of the creedal formulations of the past, we reside in a theological ghetto susceptible to the lures of any suburb where the grass looks slightly greener.

This is not the place to grapple with the massive questions of hermeneutics and historical theology. It is enough for us to note that, with all its valued contributions, inerrancy as defined by many American evangelicals, who consider themselves followers of Hodge and Warfield, is not an unmixed blessing. It has helped us treasure the biblical revelation without always helping us to hear it; it has encouraged us to study the Bible without always pointing to the right tools; it has taught us to believe the Bible without always giving us the right reasons.

Caution, therefore, is in order as to insisting on the perpetuation of the old Princeton approach to inerrancy, in its modern expression, as the only valid theological option for evangelicals. We can salute it without canonizing it. And we can seek a better approach to leave with our children, perhaps an approach that supports their belief as firmly without contorting it as markedly as the earlier view has done to our generation.

The Way Out Is the Way Back—to the Reformation

One cause of the difficulty we modern evangelicals have had in understanding the Scriptures has been our neglect of the pivotal teachings of the Reformation. Even the Christian communities that profess strong ties with the Reformers—Lutherans, Reformed churches, Presbyterian communions, Episcopalians— have not always allowed those ties to exert their steadying influence. At times the seventeenth-century scholasticism has dominated both contemporary Lutheran and Reformed theology, as is apparent in the theological discussions within the Lutheran Church-Missouri Synod and the Christian Reformed Church, through whose education system one of my ministerial friends passed without ever having read Calvin's *Institutes of the Christian Religion*! At other times the supposed sons and daughters of the Reformation have succumbed to modern, liberal expressions of the faith that Luther and Calvin would have ardently renounced.

For Baptist, Wesleyan, Anabaptist, Scandinavian Free Church, and Quaker evangelicals, the Reformation doctrinal teachings may seem even more foreign. Part of the heritage of each of these groups was to pull away from the influences of the great Protestant churches. They took with them valuable experience in devotion, courage, piety, and zeal. But their unique insights have often been gained at the expense of losing Reformation formulations of maturity and perception.

Even a cursory reading of the great evangelical creeds of the sixteenth and seventeenth centuries will suggest how much help they offer to our present question as to how we can best let the Bible be what God has intended it to be. One might argue that the fresh rediscovery of the Scriptures by the Reformers gave them a special opportunity to hear its inspired message and to discern its Spirit-given purpose. We shall do well to pick up their chief emphases and check ours by them.

The internal testimony of the Spirit may be the place to begin. The sons of the Reformation knew that they had to find a better answer to the question "How do we know the Bible is the Word of God?" than the traditional Roman Catholic one: "The Church tells us so." Coming to grips with the power of the Word that spoke creation into existence, the Word that burned uncontainably in the hearts of the prophets, the Word that prompted faith among the Gentiles as Paul preached it, the Protestants knew that what convinced us God's Word was true was the power of the same Spirit that inspired it in the beginning.[7]

This self-authenticating power of the Word is precisely what the apostolic church experienced when the Word first came: "For we know, brethren beloved by God, that he has chosen you; for our gospel came to you not only in word, but also in power and in the Holy Spirit and with full conviction" (1 Thess. 1:4–5). This note of confidence in the Spirit was given its fullest theological expression in the Westminster Confession of Faith. This document recognizes a number of the marks of sacred Scripture which identify the Bible as God's Word, yet refuses to lean unduly on any or all of them: ". . . our full persuasion and assurance of the infallible truth, and divine authority thereof, is from the inward work of the Holy Spirit, bearing witness by and with the Word in our hearts." [8]

Two points should be made on the basis of this review of Reformation teaching concerning the internal testimony of the Holy Spirit as the proof of Scripture's authority. First, we do not have to establish the trustworthiness of the Scripture before we proclaim the gospel. In a sense, the truth of the gospel takes historical priority to the truth of the Scriptures. The Word of God to prophets and apostles was truth in and of itself long before the Scriptures were completed, as the Reformed creeds often acknowledged.[9]

What proof did the prophets need to test whether God was speaking to them? Nothing but the power of that word itself.

What proof did the Thessalonians need that Paul's gospel was true? Nothing but the conviction of God the Holy Spirit. What proof do we need to know whether the Bible is the Word of God? Nothing but the Spirit of God speaking to us in Scripture.

The second point has to do with apologetics. Where the internal testimony of the Spirit is not the ground of our belief in Scripture, some other forms of argument have to be developed. Usually they are philosophical in nature. Where they are effective they plug into the philosophical mindset of their age. In the seventeenth and nineteenth centuries, *truth* was the concern, and rationalistic apologetics based roughly on Aristotle were the vogue. In our own century we have tried to cope with unbelief by pointing to the way in which God's Word brings *meaning* to an age affected by existential philosophy.

Where we recognize that our apologetic techniques must vary depending on the mindset of an era, we can use them wisely, knowing that they will have to be adjusted accordingly. The old axiom is noteworthy: the theology that weds itself to the philosophy of its age ends up a widow in the next age. We get in trouble, however, when we confuse an apologetic method with theological reality. Apologetic methods do not travel well from era to era, and the effort to take them with us may obscure God's truth at least as effectively as it defends it. Where we make the truth of the gospel dependent on the inerrancy of the Scripture, apologetics takes center stage, and all other disciplines like evangelism and Christian nurture have to wait for the text to be adequately defended.

The Holy Spirit is not plagued by such limitations. His inner witness knows the language and the need of every generation. One of his tasks in redemptive history was to inspire the Scriptures—all of them; the other was to speak to human hearts wherever those Scriptures were read and proclaimed. The Reformers knew how well the Spirit did his work. We shall gain help in our task of letting the Bible be what it is, when we follow in their train.[10]

The sufficiency of the Scriptures was another great emphasis of the sixteenth and seventeenth centuries. Tradition was not essential to doctrinal understanding. The Scriptures in and of themselves contained all that God's people needed for their Christian life and faith.[11]

In the four long centuries since Calvin and his pupil De Chandieu expressed this conviction in the French Confession of Faith (A.D. 1559), it has not been just Roman Catholic or Eastern Orthodox scholars who have treasured tradition in such a way as to compromise the sufficiency of the Scriptures. Our orthodox systems have tended to tighten themselves around the Bible to protect it. Specific interpretations of passages and precise formulations of doctrine have developed that brook no questioning even from Scripture itself.

In such cases, Scripture is in danger of being caught up in a supposedly larger system of truth which it supports and which, in turn, supports it. Thomas Aquinas's scholasticism, with its roots in Aristotle's view of reason and nature, is a case in point. So, of course, would be the uneasy marriage between idealistic philosophy and Christian revelation which characterized nineteenth-century liberalism, or the intimate liaison between existential philosophy and biblical faith which produced the theology of Bultmann and his followers. Among evangelicals, both dispensationalism, with its firm commitment to a fixed interpretation of Scripture, and the Hodge-Warfield brand of Reformed theology, with its rationalistic defense of Scripture, come close to jeopardizing the solid principle that Scripture is sufficient.

One form in which this danger shows itself in the current questions over Scripture is in the definition of *error*. As used in the delicate theological discussions in which evangelicals are now engaged, error should surely be defined in theological terms derived from and limited to the Bible itself. Yet time and again in the arguments presented by those who purport to follow the Hodge-Warfield position words like *error,* or *inerrancy,* or *infallibility* are defined by secular, twentieth-century standards, sometimes with an appeal to Webster's Dictionary for support.

We can no more define these terms from their use in common

parlance, than we can define a biblical word like *love* on the basis of a popular song, or a concept like *covenant* with the use of Anglo-Saxon law. *Error* theologically must mean that which leads us astray from the will of God or the knowledge of his truth. The notion of *error* in Scripture is too important to be trivialized as it is in danger of being in the current discussion.[12] Passages like "But who can discern his errors? Clear thou me from hidden faults" (Ps. 19:12) or "whoever brings back a sinner from the error of his way" (James 5:20) or "beware lest you be carried away with the error of lawless men" (2 Pet. 3:17) or "you are wrong [you err], because you know neither the Scriptures nor the power of God" (Matt. 22:29)—these are the scriptural uses which give us clues as to what error means.

We break with the basic Reformed teaching on the sufficiency of the Bible, both when we claim it to be inerrant on the basis of minute details of chronology, geography, history, or cosmology or when we attack its authority by pointing to alleged discrepancies. The false alternatives often posed between biblical inerrancy and biblical errancy are not themselves biblical choices.[13] They are imposed from without in a way that tries to force the Bible to give answers that God, who inspired the Book, apparently had no intention of giving.

Hermeneutical insights are another Reformation gift to the present discussions on biblical authority. Knowing how the Bible wants to be heard is as important as defending its authority. In fact, the two go inevitably and inextricably together. The Reformers tried to walk a careful line between extremes. They denied the highly private or personal interpretations of religious extremists, while rejecting the role of the church as the normative interpreter. Their commitment to *sola scriptura* made them wary of the teachings of the Fathers, the edicts of councils, or the traditions of men wherever they failed to conform to the teaching of Scripture.[14]

The principles implicit in a statement like the one on biblical interpretation in the Second Helvetic Confession (A.D. 1566) may not cover all the textbook guidelines, but they do suggest a number of essentials: (1) Scripture is its own interpreter; our beginning and ending point is what the Scripture itself says. We do not look primarily to churchly edicts, clerical opinions, or mystic visions; we take our clues from the text itself, ever mindful that behind the whole with its diversity and variety there stands God the Holy Spirit. (2) The language and setting of the various parts of Scripture must be considered. Here the way is opened for the technical, critical scholarship which the Reformation encouraged and which was virtually impossible in the Roman Catholic church, as long as it remained attached to the Latin Vulgate as the authoritative text. (3) Difficult passages are to be studied in comparison with other passages—similar and different; clear passages were to be used to shed light on less clear portions, and attention was to be given to themes that were supported by many passages. Though elements of subjectivity could not be avoided, this guideline had two great benefits: first, it kept the sons of the Reformation focused on the text of Scripture itself as the source of their spiritual wisdom; second, it provided for growth in knowledge, since an enlarged understanding of any passage made a contribution to the understanding of many other passages. The possibility of progress in scholarship and in discipleship was thus opened in a way that is not true where interpretations prevail that are fixed by scholarly edict or churchly decision. (4) The rule of faith and love was a way of assuring balance in biblical interpretation. It meant that any interpretation should be questioned that did not accord with the central themes of the faith and the crucial biblical emphasis on our love for God and one another. Petty doctrines and doubtful moral teachings were thus avoided by the controlling role that the major themes of Scripture exercised. (5) The primary purpose of the Bible had to be kept central—the glory of God through the salvation offered by Jesus Christ. Freed from the shackles of tradition and legalism, the Reformers reveled in the Word of grace which the gospel brought. They discovered afresh that the Bible was about Christ, God's Son and our Savior. Seeing him at the center held everything else the Scripture says in perspective and kept them from frittering away their attention on the irrelevant and speculative questions in which scholastic theologians, ancient and modern, have bogged themselves down.

The final Reformation insight has to do with the meaning of *the infallible rule of faith and practice.* An early reference to this phrase is found in the Belgic Confession (A.D. 1561) where the perfection of Scripture is discussed: "For since it is forbidden *to add unto or take away anything from the Word of God,* it doth thereby evidently appear that the doctrine thereof is most perfect and complete in all respects. . . . Therefore we reject with all our hearts whatsoever doth not agree with this infallible rule. . . ." [15] Two things should be noted. First, the focus is on the perfection of the *doctrine;* it is the *teaching* of Scripture that is the infallible rule. Second, that teaching is to be determined by the hermeneutical principles stated above: the comparing of Scripture with Scripture, while keeping an eye on its central teaching of salvation in Christ. The Reformers knew well that while all Scripture is inspired and, therefore, authoritative and profitable, all of it is not equally binding on God's people for their faith and obedience. Lutherans, for instance, clearly distinguished between the law which drives us to Christ and the gospel which sets us free from that law. Calvinists, while cherishing the law as the terms of the covenant in its Old Testament form, made a distinction between the ceremonial and civil laws, on the one hand, which were not binding on the Church, and the moral laws, on the other, which were binding.[16] Whereas inspiration and authority apply, then, to all the parts of Scripture, the phrase *infallible rule* should be seen as pertaining to the doctrine derived from the Scripture when it is rightly understood. Scripture is not a collection of infallible rules to be laid willy-nilly on the church without regard to setting, context, and purpose: promises given in specific circumstances cannot be generalized for the whole church; proverbs used for raising children in an ancient society are not automatically binding on Christian youths today; testimonies of personal experience in the Psalms may not always be reproduced in the lives of God's people; apostolic teachings directed to the need of an early church cannot always be applied as law in our situations without some modification: Paul's instruction to the women at Corinth about covering their heads may be an illustration (1 Cor. 11:2–16).

Every part of Scripture is God-given and, therefore, profitable. No part of it can be ignored as we seek to discern God's truth and God's will. Yet that very discernment involves a testing and a weighing of part with part, theme with theme, teaching with teaching. It is the teaching of the Book as a whole, when aptly understood, that forms the infallible rule. All parts of Scripture have their significance as they contribute to that whole. The entire mosaic gives us the picture, not just the assorted pieces.

Can we let the Bible be what it is? Can Christians cease to fault it when it does not seem to serve our standards of accuracy or speak to our scientific and historical questions? Can we let the Bible be what it is? Can Christians cease to protect it by imposing on it a rationalized defense as a guarantee of its trustworthiness? Fortunately, the Bible, as God's Word, is strong enough to survive both human attacks and human defenses. The Reformers' confidence in the Spirit's power, the Bible's sufficiency, the ability of Scripture to interpret itself, and the infallibility of its teaching can give us good help as we seek to let the Bible be what it really is.

The Way Out Is the Way Forward—to Devout Scholarship

In regard to most aspects of a doctrine of Scripture, our evangelical consensus is strong. I hear no quarrel among us about the inspiration and authority of the whole Bible. I sense no tendency to succumb to the style of liberalism that freely discounted parts of Scripture as spiritually unpalatable or morally unsavory. The impact of neo-orthodoxy's questions as to whether revelation is expressed only in encounter with God or also includes meaningful statements (propositions) about God is not impressive.

The better part of wisdom is surely for us to rally around our consensus concerning the Bible's full inspiration, while we work at some of the basic questions that need clarification. Only four such questions can be mentioned here: (1) What help can we get from fresh exegesis of the key passages that speak of inspiration and authority? (2) How can we use the methods and results of grammatical-historical-literary scholarship without repeating the errors that have plagued the church for a century? (3) How can we learn to live with differences in the interpretation and definition of inerrancy as we have with other variations in our understanding of basic doctrines? (4) What approaches can we use to keep our evangelical institutions and agencies from drifting away from a deep commitment to Scripture as God's infallible rule of faith and practice?

Fresh exegesis is an ever-recurring need in biblical studies. This is not to turn our backs on the earlier worthies of the church, from Origen to Augustine to Calvin to Westcott. It is to note that biblical scholarship is an ongoing investigation not unlike biochemistry or subatomic physics. Earlier conclusions have to be reevaluated continually. The best way to make clear our commitment to *sola scriptura* is by going to the text with the best tools we have to hear anew what it says.

Matthew 5:17–18 may be a case in point. Its strong language, ". . . till heaven and earth pass away, not an iota, not a dot, will pass from the law until all is accomplished," has frequently been used in support of the Hodge-Warfield definition of inerrancy.

The context calls this use into question. Jesus' theme is good works—better works than those of the scribes and Pharisees (5:14–16, 20). The aim of the evangelist is to highlight Jesus' teaching against any tendency toward license or antinomianism among Christians. The disciples and the fledgling community of believers were not to abandon the law; they were to outdo it, as the following paragraph indicated (5:21–48). Murder was still wrong, but in the new age anger is just as wrong (5:21–26); the command against adultery is still binding, but the new age also censures lust (5:27–30). Similar arguments follow dealing with divorce (5:31–32), swearing of vows (5:33–37), retaliation for injuries (5:38–42), love of neighbor and enemy (5:43–48).

The heart of the argument, then, is not the accuracy of Scripture but the binding, persevering quality of the divine commands that Jesus did not abolish but fulfilled. Part of that fulfillment was his work in enabling his new people to fulfill the commands —not only in letter but in spirit.

As for the strong language—"till heaven and earth pass away, not an iota, not a dot"—the context is also helpful for clarification. Hyperbole, or deliberate exaggeration for emphasis, is a device that Jesus used frequently in the Sermon on the Mount: "If your right eye causes you to sin, pluck it out and throw it away" (5:29). What can this mean but "deal drastically with sin in your life"? A literal interpretation would not only encourage self-maiming, it would surely limit the number of times that one could discipline himself in temptation! Similarly, what does Jesus' statement about the law mean but something like this? "No one of my followers should forget to keep God's commands because, transformed by my mission, they continue to regulate our lives right on into the new age."

John 10:34–36 may be another passage that deserves careful study. The parenthetical clause "and scripture cannot be broken" has been frequently cited as a key text in an evangelical view of inspiration. And with good reason: it calls attention to the binding quality of Scripture as the teaching of God.

Jesus' argument seems to focus on the authority of his citation from Psalm 82:6. The statement "scripture cannot be broken" is virtually an appeal on his part to what his Jewish opponents also believed. His aim was not to teach them new insights into the authority of Scripture, but rather to remind them of what they believed about the authority and applicability of the Scripture— an authority that made it lawful for him to be called the Son of God.

Again, we seem to get no help from this passage for our basic question: the definition of inerrancy. What we do gain is evidence that Jesus and the Jews shared a high view of the divine character of the Old Testament and of our obligation to heed its words.

2 Timothy 3:14–17 is a pivotal passage that merits intense

study as part of our evangelical agenda. The context is clearly the presence of unbelief and persecution which are the style of the present age (3:1, 10–13). Paul used his own experience to remind Timothy of how persistent, how devious, how fiendish persecution will be. Yet resources are available to help the young evangelist cope with the pressures: Paul's training and example, together with Timothy's spiritual heritage, rooted as it was in the Scriptures.

Equipment is an essential ingredient in Paul's message. Timothy had to be equipped to carry out his mission under duress. The suitable equipment was to be found in the Scriptures: (1) the message of salvation through Christ was one point of emphasis, salvation being not only Timothy's own experience but his confidence that God's whole program would triumph despite opposition; (2) the profitability of Scripture was Paul's other thrust, as he outlined its role in teaching, reproof, correction, and training in righteousness. Scripture's ability to equip is based on its inspiration. "Inspired therefore profitable to equip" was Paul's line of reasoning. Note that the emphasis here is on what the Reformers would have called the *sufficiency* and, especially, the *efficacy* of the Scripture—its power to do the work God intended it to do.

Part of what must be discussed as we seek to deal with Scripture on its own terms is the Hodge-Warfield conclusion that the Bible is inspired and *therefore* is inerrant (i.e., completely accurate) in all its details, including history, geography, chronology, and science. It is enough to say here that Paul in 2 Timothy 3 concludes, from the fact of inspiration, that Scripture is profitable and powerful. Should not this tack help us define what we mean by inerrancy, if we choose to use the word?

2 Peter 1:20–21 is another important word on inspiration. The context makes clear that there was a major conflict over *authority*. The false teachers (were they gnostics?) were putting forth a call for loyalty based on "cleverly devised myths" (1:16). In contrast, Peter grounds his message about the glorious lordship of Christ (1) in his own eyewitness experiences like the Mount of

Transfiguration and (2) in his confidence in the Old Testament prophecies that foretold the coming of the Christ.

In part the argument turns on the contrast between true prophets who are genuinely moved by God (1:20–21) and the false prophets both in antiquity and in Peter's day (2:1). The true prophets were driven by the Holy Spirit to speak for God and their speaking carried that divine authority. It is for that reason that both the authentication and the interpretation of the prophecies are God's own work, not subject to the will or whim of those trying to seduce the church.

The thrust here has to do with divine initiative in giving the Scripture and the self-authenticating force of Scripture, which needs neither private support nor private interpretation. We seem to learn nothing from 2 Peter about the definition of inerrancy which dominates the current debate.

These sketchy comments on key passages are not calculated to settle anything, but rather to suggest that careful examination of the context and intent of these and other passages is a much-needed exercise if we are to learn how the Bible wants to be heard as it speaks about itself.

Openness to biblical scholarship along with fresh exegesis is another desirable attitude we must cultivate if we are going to take Scripture on its own terms. No effective exegesis can be done without this.

Our generation has better tools and resources available than any generation since the biblical period. We have begun to understand not only how the Hebrews lived but how they felt and thought, thanks to the insights of anthropology and sociology. We can reconstruct in some detail the importance of clan relationships, their attitudes toward creation and worship, their understanding of history and the covenant God made with them within it, because of the progress made in biblical theology. We have a much better grasp of the why and the to-whom of the Gospels, thanks to redaction-criticism, an approach to a biblical book that studies how and why it was written in its final form. Our knowledge of life in the cities of Paul has shed valuable light on the purpose of his epistles. Meanings of words, cultural and historical references, allusions to pagan ideas and practices—these have all been illuminated by the patient work of hundreds of scholars, some of whom have helped us recover the most reliable Greek texts for each document.

Perhaps two other gains are even more important. For one, the attitude of the men and women who study the Bible technically in our day is directed much more to the understanding of the Bible's teaching than to the undercutting of it. The harmful results of the aggressive teachers who sought to strip Scripture of its divinity half a century and more ago have, in many cases, been replaced by a large measure of appreciation for the biblical revelation. For another gain, we are much more aware today of the dangers of imposing a philosophy on the Scripture—like Wellhausen's evolutionary approach to the development of Israel's religion or Bultmann's existential understanding of the meaning of Christian faith and life.

This does not mean that we can glibly accept all the results of biblical scholarship. It does not mean that liberal, unbelieving scholars have vanished. It does mean that we can be open to the use of all tools and resources. And we can be open to them not as a grudging concession to creeping liberalism, but as the valid —indeed the God-ordained—means of determining the God-inspired meaning of the text. Carl F. H. Henry ("Agenda for Evangelical Advance") has called for a renewed vigor in American evangelical scholarship, which has been overdependent on Britain and Europe. I cannot speak for the scholars who specialize in philosophical or systematic theology. But I have a hunch that one explanation accounts for the silence of evangelical *biblical* scholars more than any other: the basic fear that their findings, as they deal with the text of Scripture, will conflict with the popular understanding of what inerrancy entails. Where a rigid system of apologetics becomes the basic definition of orthodoxy, true biblical scholarship becomes difficult if not impossible.

Can we in our evangelical institutions begin to enjoy the freedom to give public expression to the results of our scholarship?

No evangelical constituency or administration should value safety more than truth and accuracy in biblical interpretation. Without freedom responsibly used, we will be incapable of leaving to our generation a legacy of biblical learning anything like what the evangelical scholars of the nineteenth century left to us.

It may be well for us to keep in mind that the conclusions to which we come as to the meaning and intent of a book or passage may disagree with the tradition in which we have been raised. This should come as no surprise to us who believe in human sin and human limitations. And it should surprise least of all those of us who are heirs of the Reformation, with its insistence that Scripture has priority over the teachings of the fathers—even, on occasion, our own evangelical fathers.

But our gains can be immense. Devout and cautious use of all the tools and insights possible will be one of the great gifts of providence to Christ's church. With patience, intelligence, and prayer, we will be able to look inside the life and faith of our biblical forebears with an accuracy and a perception that will bring true knowledge to our generation and glory to God's name. The way out of our impasse in understanding is both back and forward.

Living with our differences is a monumental lesson to be learned. By and large our generation of evangelicals has not done badly. In Billy Graham crusades for more than twenty-five years, we have set aside our differences in the definition of evangelism and gotten on with the task of pointing men and women to Christ. In mission gatherings like those at Berlin (1966) and Lausanne (1974) we have prayed and planned together about world evangelization despite conflicts in matters like the relationship between church growth and social action.

And we have a heritage that has surmounted theological controversy to form Bible societies, mission boards, campus ministries, rescue missions, and interdenominational Bible schools, colleges, and seminaries.

Anglicans and Baptists, Methodists and Lutherans have affirmed each other's rights to be called evangelical despite major differences in views of church government and the sacraments. The bitter Reformation debates between Luther's followers and Calvin's concerning the nature of Christ's presence in the communion have long since cooled, as have the sharp disagreements between them on the precise manner in which Christ's humanity and deity relate to each other in the incarnation.

With so much to gain from cooperation, and with so much to lose in understanding and insight from hostility, the time has long since come for evangelicals to accept their differences in the precise formulation of views of infallibility and inerrancy. The opportunism that finds one evangelical church agency or institution claiming to hold a higher view of Scripture than others is scarcely worthy of Christ's kingdom. The possibility for our motivation to go sour in such rivalry is so great that we ought to lean over backwards to avoid it. To recruit students or rally support or withhold fellowship over a definition of biblical inerrancy or the appropriateness of using the term seems futile, if not wicked.

Surely we need our best minds and spirits working on such questions. That work will have a much better chance of success in the clear air of fellowship than in an atmosphere fouled by competition.

Where evangelical affirmations—the triune nature of God, the true humanity and deity of the Christ, his virgin birth, vicarious death, bodily resurrection, glorious ascension, and personal coming, the reality of the Spirit's mission in the church, the need for conversion and new life, the call to discipleship and participation in the tasks of world evangelization and social action—are shared, let these be the ground of unity.

The questions, as I hear them, do not turn on whether the Bible is errant or not. Biblical errancy is not an option for most evangelicals. The questions are: (1) Is inerrancy the best word to use to describe the Bible's infallibility and truthfulness? (2) If inerrancy is to be used, how do we define it in a way that accords with the teachings and the data of Scripture? That is an important agenda, but one far too limited for us to divide over.

Evangelical variety seems to be evident even in the ways our doctrines of Scripture are phrased. A thorough examination of the official doctrinal statements of our evangelical agencies and schools would reveal a number of patterns which have been used to express a firm commitment to Scripture's unique character.

Some organizations employ a specific statement about the inerrancy of the original documents: "We believe that the Bible, consisting of the Old and New Testaments only, is verbally inspired by the Holy Spirit, is inerrant in the original manuscripts, and is the infallible and authoritative Word of God" (Interdenominational Foreign Mission Association).

Others specifically apply the concept of inerrancy to the rule or guidance that Scripture gives: "We receive the Bible in its entirety, and the Bible alone, as the Word of God written, and therefore the inerrant rule of faith and practice" (Inter-Varsity Christian Fellowship).

It is worth noting that the National Association of Evangelicals chose the word "infallibility" rather than inerrancy for its statement: ". . . we believe the Bible to be the inspired, the only infallible, authoritative word of God."

Perhaps more surprising is the fact that the center of the doctrinal stance of one of the great Bible schools of our land is on verbal inspiration, with no mention of inerrancy: "The Bible, including both the Old and New Testaments, is a divine revelation, the original autographs of which were verbally inspired by the Holy Spirit" (Moody Bible Institute).

This brief sampling of doctrinal statements suggests that we have lived with variety for some time in the way we express our commitment to Scripture. Perhaps we should continue to enjoy this variety, while we go back to the text to hear afresh what God is saying.[17]

Guidelines for evangelical constancy are a further topic for discussion. Whether or not we accept the "domino theory" that suggests that the drift toward liberalism begins when a view of inerrancy akin to that of Hodge and Warfield is given up, concern for evangelical constancy is something that we all should share.

Creedal affirmations are important. Christian agencies do well to have sufficient consensus on the fundamentals of the faith to make their purposes clear and to keep them stable.

Institutional or churchly discipline also needs to be exercised in the selection and retention of key personnel. Careful screening and periodic review should be part of this discipline. Whatever range of theological expression is present must be tested by the norm of the Scripture and by the organization's statement of faith.

Vital experiences of worship and fellowship are also necessary. Whatever Christian theology may be, it is never purely academic. It is unto nurture and worship. Openness to the renewing Spirit of God is certainly one mark of what it means to be evangelical.

If the Protestant principle of *sola scriptura* is to be honored, statements of faith should be subject to periodic review and occasional change. This is especially true when special, unwritten interpretations have grown up around the statements. Such traditions can become dangerous. If they are not crucial, they should be dropped; if they are, they should be incorporated into the official statement.

Inasmuch as the historic creeds of the church have rarely spelled out a full doctrine of Scripture, and almost never of inerrancy, it is better for us to judge the evangelical orthodoxy of our brothers and sisters by the adherence to the great evangelical doctrines—like those of the *Fundamentals* (1910–1911) or the appropriate classical evangelical creeds—than by the use or nonuse of specific phrases or catch words.

In the long run, what has to be weighed is the impact of a colleague's ministry on those whom his life touches. It is possible for a person to be creedally correct and still have a negative impact because of pride, rigidity, or spiritual shallowness. And it is possible for a person to struggle inadequately with precise doctrinal wording and still make a wholesome impact on those whom he serves through his devotion to the Word and his firm Christian faith.

Maybe all of this is asking too much. Can we understand the

mixed impact that the narrow, precise definition of inerrancy has had on evangelical vitality? Can we take the road back to the Reformation to remind ourselves of how far we have moved in our ways of defending and interpreting Scripture? Can we begin discussion afresh on our exegesis of key passages, our openness to the methods of historical research, our tolerance of detailed differences in doctrine, our approaches to assuring our continuity as evangelicals?

None of this is easy. Almost all of it will carry pain. Yet the stakes are high. As evangelicals, hearing the Bible is our highest priority. That is best done not in the clamor of battle but in the quiet of diligent study, firm fellowship, and fervent prayer.

NOTES

THE CHURCH DOCTRINE OF BIBLICAL AUTHORITY

1. John 14:26. See Geoffrey W. Bromiley, "The Church Doctrine of Inspiration," *Revelation and the Bible,* ed. Carl F. H. Henry (Grand Rapids: Baker Book House, 1958), p. 205. This article is perhaps still the best brief overview of the history of the doctrine of inspiration.

2. J. N. D. Kelly, *Early Christian Doctrines* (New York: Harper & Row, 1960), pp. 52–53.

3. Bernhard Lohse, *A Short History of Christian Doctrine,* trans. F. Ernest Stoeffler (Philadelphia: Fortress Press, 1966), p. 28.

4. I am indebted throughout this article to Donald K. McKim, a doctoral student in church history at Pittsburgh Theological Seminary, for his collaboration. He has shared his insights and much unpublished research material, in this case a paper entitled "The Doctrine of Scripture in Origen and Its Use in the Commentary on John" (1972). See R. P. C. Hanson, *Origen's Doctrine of Tradition* (London: SPCK, 1954), p. 33.

5. Jean Danielou, *Origen,* trans. Walter Mitchell (New York: Sheed and Ward, 1955), pp. 74, 80.

6. Charles Bigg, *The Christian Platonists of Alexandria* (Oxford: Clarendon Press, 1886), p. 155.

7. Origen, "De Principiis," trans. F. Crombie, *The Ante-Nicene Fathers,* Vol. IV, ed. Alexander Roberts and James Donaldson (Buffalo: Christian Literature Publishing Company, 1885; American reprint of the Edinburgh edition), IV, 9; IV, 8, pp. 356–57.

8. R. P. C. Hanson, *Allegory and Event* (Richmond: John Knox Press, 1959), pp. 198 ff.

9. F. W. Farrar, *History of Interpretation* (New York: Dutton, 1886), p. 190.

10. Farrar, p. 190.

11. Hanson, *Allegory,* p. 226.

12. Bruce Vawter, *Biblical Inspiration* (Philadelphia: Westminster Press, 1972), p. 40.

13. Cited in G. C. Berkouwer, *Holy Scripture,* trans. Jack B. Rogers (Grand Rapids: Eerdmans, 1975), pp. 175–76.

14. Peter Brown, *Augustine of Hippo* (London: Faber, 1967), pp. 91–95.

15. Cited in John E. Smith, *The Analogy of Experience* (New York: Harper & Row, 1973), p. 8.

16. Cited in Robert F. Davidson, ed., *The Search for Meaning in Life* (New York: Holt, Rinehart and Winston, 1962), p. 292.

17. Smith, pp. 9–10.

18. Cited in E. L. Miller, ed., *Classical Statements on Faith and Reason* (New York: Random House, 1970), p. 36.

19. Vawter, p. 33.

20. R. M. Grant, *The Letter and the Spirit* (London: SPCK, 1957), p. 108.

21. Vawter, pp. 38–39.

22. Cited in A. D. R. Polman, *The Word of God According to St. Augustine,* trans. A. J. Pomerans (Grand Rapids: Eerdmans, 1961), p. 49.

23. Polman, pp. 59–60.

24. Polman, p. 57.

25. Augustin Bea, *The Study of the Synoptic Gospels,* English version ed. Joseph A. Fitzmeyer (New York: Harper & Row, 1965), p. 59.

26. Cited in Raymond Larry Shelton, "Martin Luther's Concept of Biblical Interpretation in Historical Perspective" (Ph.D. diss., Fuller Theological Seminary, 1974), p. 109.

27. Miller, p. 41.

28. Otto W. Heick, *A History of Christian Thought,* vol. 1 (Philadelphia: Fortress Press, 1965), pp. 300–303.

29. Shelton, p. 147.

30. Shelton, pp. 120–21.

31. Cited in Hugh Thompson Kerr, Jr., ed., *A Compend of Luther's Theology* (Philadelphia: Westminster Press, 1943), p. 4.

32. Kerr, p. 3.

33. Kerr, p. 9.

34. Kerr, p. 11.

35. Willem Jan Kooiman, *Luther and the Bible,* trans. John Schmidt (Philadelphia: Muhlenberg Press, 1961), p. 237.

36. Shelton, p. 179.

37. John Calvin, *Institutes of the Christian Religion,* ed. J. T. McNeill, trans. F. L. Battles (Philadelphia: Westminster Press, 1960), I, iii, 1; hereafter cited as *Inst.*

38. *Inst.,* I, iii, 1.

39. *Inst.,* I, iii, 3.

40. *Inst.,* I, iv, 1.

41. *Inst.,* I, iii, 1.

42. *Inst.,* I, vi, 1.

43. *Inst.,* I, vi, 1.

44. *Inst.,* I, vi, 1.

45. *Inst.,* I, vii, 1.

46. *Inst.,* I, vii, 2.

47. *Inst.,* I, vii, 4.

48. *Inst.,* I, viii, 13.

49. *Inst.,* I, viii, 13.

50. *Inst.,* I, ix, 3.

51. *Inst.,* I, ix, 3.

52. *Inst.,* III, ii, 1.

53. 1 Peter 1:21 in John Calvin, *Hebrews and the First and Second Epistles of St. Peter,* trans. William B. Johnston, ed. D. W. and T. F. Torrance (Grand Rapids: Eerdmans, 1963), p. 250.

54. *Inst.,* I, xiii, 1.

55. *Inst.,* I, xvii, 13. The context here is a passage of Scripture where God is said to repent.

56. Romans 3:4 in John Calvin, *The Epistles of Paul the Apostle to the Romans and to the Thessalonians,* trans. R. Mackenzie, ed. D. W. and T. F. Torrance (Grand Rapids: Eerdmans, 1961), p. 61.

57. Hebrews 10:6 in Calvin, *Hebrews,* p. 136.

58. Genesis 1:15,16 in John Calvin, *The First Book of Moses Called Genesis,* trans. John King (Grand Rapids: Eerdmans, 1948), pp. 86–87. Cited in Arthur Lindsley, "The Principle of Accommodation" (unpublished paper, Pittsburgh Theological Seminary, 1975), pp. 17–18.

59. T. H. L. Parker, *John Calvin: A Biography* (Philadelphia: Westminster Press, 1975), p. 77.

60. For the evidence regarding Beza see Brian G. Armstrong, *Calvinism and the Amyraut Heresy* (Madison: University of Wisconsin Press, 1969), pp. 38–42.

61. Armstrong, p. 32, notes that Protestant Scholasticism "is more a spirit, an attitude of life, than a list of beliefs." He lists, however,

four "more-or-less identifiable tendencies." Cf. Bromiley in *Revelation and the Bible,* pp. 213–14, who points to five "shifts of emphasis" from the teaching of the Reformers which are "slight in themselves but serious in their historical consequences."

62. Robert P. Scharlemann, *Thomas Aquinas and John Gerhard* (New Haven: Yale University Press, 1964), p. 4.

63. Leon McDill Allison, "The Doctrine of Scripture in the Theology of John Calvin and Francis Turretin" (Th.M. thesis, Princeton Theological Seminary, 1958), p. 57. All citations from Turretin's *Institutio* are taken from this most helpful study.

64. Allison, pp. 59–60.

65. Allison, p. 60.

66. Allison, p. 60.

67. Allison, p. 61.

68. Allison, p. 61.

69. Allison, p. 62.

70. Allison, p. 92.

71. Donald D. Grohman, "The Genevan Reactions to the Samur Doctrine of Hypothetical Universalism: 1635–1685" (Th.D. diss., Knox College, Toronto, 1971), pp. 380–84.

72. Grohman, pp. 432–33. The English translation of the *Consensus* is by Archibald Alexander Hodge in *Outlines of Theology* (1897; reprint ed. Grand Rapids: Eerdmans, 1949) and reprinted in John H. Leith, ed., *Creeds of the Churches* (Richmond: John Knox Press, rev. ed., 1973).

73. John W. Beardslee, ed. and trans., *Reformed Dogmatics* (New York: Oxford University Press, 1965), p. 5.

74. Jack Bartlett Rogers, *Scripture in the Westminster Confession* (Grand Rapids: Eerdmans, 1967), chap. 3. This work, now out of print, will be reissued in 1977 by Acton House, 1888 Century Park East, Los Angeles, CA 90067.

75. Rogers, pp. 87–89. I am also indebted to Donald K. McKim, "Ramist Influence on Amesian Methodology" (unpublished paper, Pittsburgh Theological Seminary, 1975).

76. Rogers, pp. 90, 237–38.

77. Cited in Rogers, p. 247.

78. Rogers, p. 267. A helpful and historically reliable treatment of the Westminster divines' views on the Bible is contained in John H. Leith, *Assembly at Westminster* (Richmond: John Knox Press, 1973).

79. Rogers, p. 312.

80. Rogers, p. 321.

81. Rogers, pp. 366, 367.

82. Rogers, pp. 426–27.

83. Rogers, p. 324.

84. Rogers, p. 323.

85. Donald K. McKim, "John Owen's Doctrine of Scripture in Historical Perspective," *The Evangelical Quarterly* (Oct.-Dec., 1973), pp. 195–207. McKim points out that Owen was a transitional figure, in most ways maintaining a Reformation stance, while at points giving in to rationalist tendencies.

86. Rogers, p. 149.

87. Lefferts A. Loetscher, *The Broadening Church* (Philadelphia: University of Pennsylvania Press, 1954), chap. 1.

88. I have been helped in developing this section by Donald K. McKim, "Archibald Alexander and the Doctrine of Scripture," *Journal of Presbyterian History* 54, no. 3 (Fall 1976): 355–75; hereafter cited as "Alexander."

89. James W. Alexander, *The Life of Archibald Alexander, D.D.* (New York: Charles Scribner, 1854), pp. 108–109; hereafter cited as *LAA*.

90. *LAA*, p. 368.

91. A. A. Hodge, *The Life of Charles Hodge, D.D., LL.D.* (New York: Charles Scribner's Sons, 1880), p. 323.

92. I have been immeasurably helped in understanding the theological and especially the philosophical background of A. A. Alexander and Charles Hodge by an unpublished paper of John W. Stewart, "The Princeton Theologians: The Tethered Theology" (dissertation research in preparation for the Department of History at the University of Michigan, 1975).

93. Stewart, p. 9.

94. Archibald Alexander, *Evidences of the Authenticity, Inspiration, and Canonical Authority of the Holy Scriptures* (Philadelphia: Presbyterian Board of Publication, 1836), p. 229.

95. Charles Hodge, *Systematic Theology*, vol. 1 (New York: Charles Scribner & Company, 1872–73), p. 152; hereafter cited as *ST*.

96. *ST*, p. 163.

97. Archibald A. Hodge and Benjamin B. Warfield, "Inspiration," *The Presbyterian Review* (April 1881), p. 238; hereafter cited as *PR*.

98. *PR*, p. 245.

99. *PR*, p. 245.

100. Charles Hodge, "What Is Christianity?" *The Biblical Repertory and Princeton Review* (January 1860), p. 121.

101. Stewart, p. 17.

102. Stewart, pp. 17–18.

103. *The Works of John Witherspoon, D.D.,* VI (Edinburgh: 1815), p. 22, cited in McKim, "Alexander," p. 359.

104. *ST,* p. 134.

105. Stewart, p. 25.

106. Rogers, p. 29.

107. See Rogers, *Scripture in the Westminster Confession,* pp. 28–43, and Loetscher, *The Broadening Church,* pp. 29–62.

108. Rogers, p. 31.

109. Loetscher, p. 61.

110. Rogers, p. 49.

111. Maurice Armstrong et al., eds., *The Presbyterian Enterprise* (Philadelphia: Westminster Press, 1956), p. 286.

112. Loetscher, p. 135.

113. See James Orr, *Revelation and Inspiration* (New York: Charles Scribner's Sons, 1910; republished 1952), pp. 199, 212–17.

114. Berkouwer, *Holy Scripture,* p. 9; hereafter cited as *HS.*

115. Herman Bavinck, *Gereformeerde Dogmatick,* vol. 1 (Kampen: J. H. Kok, 1928), p. 411; hereafter cited as *GD.* All translations are mine from the Dutch fourth edition.

116. Cited in *GD,* p. 415.

117. *GD,* p. 420.

118. *GD,* p. 419.

119. *GD,* p. 417.

120. Abraham Kuyper, *Principles of Sacred Theology,* trans. J. Hendrik DeVries (Grand Rapids: Eerdmans, 1968), pp. 556–57.

121. *GD,* p. 414.

122. *GD,* p. 409.

123. *HS,* p. 181.

124. *HS,* p. 183.

125. *HS,* p. 183.

126. *HS,* p. 180.

127. See Harold Lindsell, *The Battle for the Bible* (Grand Rapids: Zondervan, 1976), pp. 18, 19, 27, for such a claim.

128. See John Gerstner, "The Theological Boundaries of Evangelical Faith," *The Evangelicals,* ed. David F. Wells and John D. Woodbridge (Nashville: Abingdon Press, 1975), pp. 21–37, for such a claim.

129. See Francis Schaeffer, *Escape from Reason* (London: Inter-Varsity Fellowship, 1968), p. 35, for an example of this kind of uncritical commitment to Aristotelian thought forms.

130. As Clark Pinnock in his essay in this volume and elsewhere seeks to do.

THREE VIEWS OF THE BIBLE IN CONTEMPORARY THEOLOGY

1. For the sake of brevity, I have had reluctantly to omit the most instructive Roman Catholic discussion of these matters. Like conservative evangelicals, Roman Catholics have been struggling to balance an official position on biblical infallibility with fresh critical insight into the phenomena of Scripture. Thus their debate is quite analogous to our own. See Bruce Vawter, *Biblical Inspiration* (Philadelphia: Westminster, 1971) and James T. Burchaell, *Catholic Theories of Biblical Inspiration since 1810* (Cambridge: University Press, 1969).

2. L. Harold DeWolf, *A Theology of the Living Church* (New York: Harper & Row, 1953, rev. ed. 1960).

3. Cf. L. Harold DeWolf, *The Case for Theology in Liberal Perspective* (Philadelphia: Westminster, 1959), pp. 46–59.

4. Gordon D. Kaufman, "What Shall We Do with the Bible?," *Interpretation* 25 (1971), pp. 95 f. To much the same effect, cf. Wolfhart Pannenberg, "The Crisis of the Scripture Principle," *Basic Questions in Theology,* vol. 1 (Philadelphia: Fortress Press, 1970), pp. 1–14.

5. James Barr, *The Bible in the Modern World* (London: SCM, 1973).

6. C. F. Evans, *Is 'Holy Scripture' Christian?* (London: SCM, 1971).

7. DeWolf, *A Theology of the Living Church,* pp. 75–86.

8. Schubert M. Ogden, *The Reality of God* (New York: Harper & Row, 1966), p. 190.

9. Cited in Harry E. Fosdick, *The Modern Use of the Bible* (New York: Macmillan, 1924), p. 2.

10. Cf. Barth, *Church Dogmatics* 1/2, chap. 3, "Holy Scripture."

11. Barth, *Baptism as the Foundation of the Christian Life* (Edinburgh: T. & T. Clark, 1969), p. 107.

12. Barth, *Church Dogmatics* III/1, p. 23.

13. Cf. Paul K. Jewett, *Emil Brunner's Concept of Revelation* (London: James Clarke, 1954), pp. 117 f.

14. Barth, *Church Dogmatics* I/2, pp. 529 f.

15. Barth, *Church Dogmatics* I/2, pp. 507–510.

16. Barth, *Evangelical Theology: An Introduction* (New York: Holt, Rinehart and Winston, 1963), pp. 29 f.

17. Barth, *Church Dogmatics* I/1, pp. 139, 157; I/2, pp. 513, 525.

18. Barth, *Church Dogmatics* I/2, pp. 507 f.

19. Barth, *Church Dogmatics* I/2, p. 688.

20. On this motif of freedom in the new reformation view, see K. Runia, *Karl Barth's Doctrine of Holy Scripture* (Grand Rapids: Eerdmans, 1962), pp. 189–219.

21. Bultmann, *Existence and Faith* (New York: World, 1960), p. 85.

22. John Baillie, *The Idea of Revelation in Recent Thought* (New York: Columbia University Press, 1956), pp. 28, 33, 39, 47.

23. Still unsurpassed is Bernard Ramm, *Special Revelation and the Word of God* (Grand Rapids: Eerdmans, 1961).

24. B. B. Warfield, *The Inspiration and Authority of the Bible* (Philadelphia: Presbyterian and Reformed, 1948), pp. 131–66. More recently, J. W. Wenham has expanded upon the case as it relates to Jesus and his view of inspiration: *Christ and the Bible* (Chicago: Inter-Varsity, 1973).

25. Most recently, Leon Morris, *I Believe in Revelation* (Grand Rapids: Eerdmans, 1976), chaps. 3, 8.

26. Gerrit C. Berkouwer, *Holy Scripture* (Grand Rapids: Eerdmans, 1975), chap. 1.

27. Warfield, *Inspiration and Authority,* pp. 173, 420.

28. James Orr, *Revelation and Inspiration* (Grand Rapids: Eerdmans, 1952), pp. 212–17; Berkouwer, *Holy Scripture,* p. 265. Cf. Richard J. Coleman, "Biblical Inerrancy: Are We Going Anywhere?," *Theology Today* 33 (1976), pp. 295–303; Dewey M. Beegle, *Scripture, Tradition, and Infallibility* (Grand Rapids: Eerdmans, 1973).

29. A review of some of these questions and issues which I have found helpful is to be found in a forthcoming book by Stephen T. Davis, *The Debate about the Bible: Inerrancy versus Infallibility* (Philadelphia: Westminster, 1977).

30. "No objection [to inerrancy] is valid which overlooks the prime question: what was the professed or implied purpose of the writer in making this statement?" B. B. Warfield and A. A. Hodge, *The Presbyterian Review* 6 (1881): 245.

31. So E. F. Harrison, "The Phenomena of Scripture," in *Revelation and the Bible,* Carl F. H. Henry, ed. (Grand Rapids: Baker, 1958), p. 238.

32. Harold Lindsell, *The Battle for the Bible* (Grand Rapids: Zondervan, 1976), p. 18.

33. In addition to Lindsell, see also F. A. Schaeffer, *No Final Conflict* (Downers Grove, Ill.: Inter-Varsity Press, 1975), p. 9.

34. Orr, *Revelation and Inspiration,* p. 198.

35. According to E. J. Carnell, *The Case for Orthodox Theology* (Philadelphia: Westminster, 1959), p. 106.

36. As I tried to do in *Biblical Revelation* (Chicago: Moody Press, 1971), chap. 5.

37. The poor rooster to Lindsell's mind had to crow six times to make inerrant sense out of Peter's denial story! (*Battle for the Bible,* pp. 174–76).

38. Roman Catholics, working with their inherited doctrine of inerrancy, have been more imaginative than we have, and evangelicals would benefit from considering the ideas they have come up with. Cf. Bruce Vawter, *Biblical Inspiration* (Philadelphia: Westminster, 1971).

39. Lindsell, *Battle for the Bible,* p. 210. Calling our evangelical heritage a "badge" is not a happy way of referring to it.

40. Beegle, *Scripture, Tradition and Infallibility,* pp. 69–76, 81 f., 85, 265, 279 f.

41. In fairness to Dr. Jewett, it may be that my judgments as to his theological method are exaggerated on the dark side. He may only be intending to say that the difficult texts, though divinely intended as part of the Word of God, do not possess normative authority for Christians today. If this should prove to be so, the problem would be considerably lessened.

42. For checking at least some of my folly in this essay I am grateful to the faculty of Regent College, in particular Dr. Ian S. Rennie.

43. James D. Smart, *The Strange Silence of the Bible in the Church* (Philadelphia: Westminster, 1970), p. 9.

THE BIBLE'S OWN APPROACH TO AUTHORITY

1. Cf. C. Duraisngh, "The Authority of Scripture in the Modern Period," *The Indian Journal of Theology* 23, nos. 1 & 2 (January-June 1974): 61.

2. Ibid., pp. 76–77.

3. On God's pathos, see Abraham Joshua Heschel, *The Prophets,* 2 vols. (New York: Harper & Row, Harper Torchbooks, 1969, 1971), 2:1–103, 263–72.

4.. Harold Lindsell, *The Battle for the Bible* (Grand Rapids: Zondervan, 1976), pp. 30–31.

5. See G. C. Berkouwer, *Studies in Dogmatics: Holy Scripture* (Grand Rapids: Eerdmans, 1975), p. 181. Berkouwer contends that technical incorrectness is not equated with deception in the biblical definition of error.

6. Gottfried Quell and Werner Foerster, *"kurios* family," in *Theological Dictionary of the New Testament,* ed. Gerhard Kittel and Gerhard Friedrich, trans. Geoffrey Bromiley, 9 vols. (Grand Rapids: Eerdmans, 1965), 3:1039–98. (Major divisions: Old Testament, Quell, 3:1058–81; Greek background, Later Judaism, New Testament, Foerster, 3:1039–58, 1081–98.) On Lord for Yahweh, see 3:1059. On "I am . . . ," see 3:1073.

7. Gerhard Delling, *"plēroō,"* in *Theological Dictionary of the New Testament,* 6:293–94.

8. Joachim Jeremias, *"Kleis,"* in *Theological Dictionary of the New Testament,* 3:751–52. See the whole section, 3:749–52.

9. Cf. Walter Grundmann on the use of prepositions with the term *Christ. "Christos,"* in *Theological Dictionary of the New Testament,* 9:550.

THE PASTOR AS A BIBLICAL CHRISTIAN

1. Joachim Jeremias, "The Present Position in the Controversy Concerning the Problem of the Historical Jesus," *Expository Times* (1958), p. 333.

2. Karl Barth, *Dogmatics in Outline* (New York: Harper & Row, 1956), pp. 12, 13. "Dogmatics is a critical science. So it cannot be held, as is sometimes thought, that it is a matter of stating certain old or even new propositions that one can take home in black and white. On the contrary, if there exists a critical science at all, which is constantly having to begin at the beginning, dogmatics is that science. Outwardly, of course, dogmatics arises from the fact that the Church's proclamation is in danger of going astray. Dogmatics is the testing of Church doctrine and proclamation, not an arbitrary testing from a freely chosen standpoint, but from the standpoint of the Church which in this case is the solely relevant standpoint. The concrete significance of this is that dogmatics measures the Church's proclamation by the standard of the Holy Scriptures, of the Old and New Testaments. Holy Scripture is the document of the basis, of the innermost life of the Church, the document of the manifestation of the Word of God in the person of Jesus Christ. We have no other document for this living basis of the Church; and where the Church is alive, it will always be having to reassess itself by this standard. We cannot pursue dogmatics without this standard being kept in sight. We must always be putting the question, 'What is the evidence?' Not the evidence of my thoughts, or my heart, but the evidence of

the apostles and prophets, as the evidence of God's self-evidence. Should a dogmatics lose sight of this standard, it would be an irrelevant dogmatics."

3. John Calvin, *Institutes of the Christian Religion,* ed. J. T. McNeill, trans. F. L. Battles (Philadelphia: Westminster Press, 1960), p. 590.

4. The textual evidence supports verses 31–36 as the continuation of John the Baptist's speech. See Calvin, C. K. Barrett.

5. Martin Luther, *Luther's Works,* Vol. 54, ed. Theodore Tappert (Philadelphia: Fortress Press, 1967), p. 445.

6. *Luther's Works,* Vol. 54, p. 42.

7. T. W. Manson, *Studies in the Gospels and Epistles* (Manchester: University Press, 1962).

8. Ernest Renan, *The Life of Jesus* (New York: Belmont-Tower, 1972), and David F. Strauss, *The Life of Jesus Critically Examined,* 2 vols. (Philadelphia: Fortress Press, 1972), are examples of this methodology.

9. Ernst Käsemann, *New Testament Questions Today* (London: SCM, 1969).

10. As I preach a series of expository sermons on a book of the Bible, it is my usual practice to distribute an inductive study guide to the book for small group or individual Bible study.

11. Ernst Käsemann, *Jesus Means Freedom* (Philadelphia: Fortress Press, 1974).

THE CURRENT TENSIONS: IS THERE A WAY OUT?

1. There were other factors, of course, like the influence of Philo and rabbinic exegesis, which contributed to the ascendancy of the allegorical method. But without the concerted attacks on the Old Testament by Marcion and others, it is doubtful that the allegorical method would have hardened into the dominant system of interpretation that it became. For a brief discussion of the hermeneutical conflicts, see D. A. Hubbard, "Old Testament," *The New International Dictionary of the Christian Church* (Grand Rapids: Zondervan, 1974), pp. 725 ff.

2. Illustrations of this are found in Harold Lindsell's *The Battle for the Bible* (Grand Rapids: Zondervan, 1976): (1) Lindsell connects the verse

"When the morning stars sang together,
and all the sons of God shouted for joy?" (Job 38:7, RSV)

with the scientific discovery that "there is music that comes from the stars" (p. 38). Apparently he sees this as an improvement over an interpretation that views this as figurative language. His desire to find scientific support obscures for him the poetry of the passage, whose true intent is to remind Job that he was not around when the universe burst forth in celebration at the founding of the earth, just as music blessed the rebuilding of the Temple (Ezra 3:10, 11). (2) Lindsell struggles to harmonize the accounts of Peter's denial as found in the four Gospels, each of which quotes Jesus as warning Peter that he will deny the Master three times. Because of slight variations in the text, Lindsell is forced to conclude that there were two separate warnings of three denials each, with the result that Peter actually denied his Lord six times. If such harmonization were the Holy Spirit's aim, it is difficult to know why he gave us four separate Gospels instead of one.

3. "Higher criticism," of course, is an absolutely essential discipline which asks basic questions of the biblical documents: When were they written, to whom, and by whom? What human circumstances and processes of composition or editing did the Holy Spirit use as he inspired the books of the Bible? Higher criticism complements "lower criticism," the attempt to recover the text of the Scripture that comes as close as possible to the original manuscripts.

4. Francis Steele in *Christianity Today,* April 9, 1976, p. 35.

5. This is not to say that the Bible is full of inaccuracies. Indeed, it is highly accurate, especially when we define its accuracy not in terms of foreign standards but in terms of the authors' purposes. Imposing contemporary standards of accuracy contributes little to our understanding of the text. Lindsell's concern that the Bible be found "free from errors in matters of fact, science, history, and chronology, as well as in matters having to do with salvation" (*Battle for the Bible,* p. 107) is a case in point. This statement immediately prompts questions like, Whose standards of historical accuracy? What scientific framework? Which chronological reconstruction? Is it sound theology to ask the Bible to conform to the relative and changing standards of our academic disciplines?

6. An illustration of this comes from Francis Schaeffer's otherwise helpful notes on *Genesis in Space and Time* (Downers Grove, Ill.: Inter-Varsity Press, 1972), where he rightly points out the non-mythological nature of Genesis. Yet he pays almost no attention to the literary character of Genesis as an ancient oriental book that must be read on its own terms, and he comments not at all on the circumstances in the life of Israel which God used to give rise to Genesis. In other words, the other half of the space-time question,

the space and time in which the book was composed, is virtually ignored.

7. "We know these books to be canonical, and the sure rule of our faith, not so much by the common accord and consent of the Church, as by the testimony and inward illumination of the Holy Spirit, which enables us to distinguish them from other ecclesiastical books upon which, however useful, we cannot find any articles of faith" ("The French Confession of Faith" [A.D. 1559], in Philip Schaff, *The Creeds of Christendom* [New York: 1877], 3:361–62).

8. The preceding section of the Westminster Confession reads as follows: "We may be moved and induced by the testimony of the Church to an high and reverent esteem of the Holy Scripture; and the heavenliness of the matter, the efficacy of the doctrine; the majesty of the style, the consent of all the parts, the scope of the whole (which is to give all glory to God), the full discovery it makes of the only way of man's salvation, the many other incomparable excellencies, and the entire perfection there of, are arguments whereby it doth abundantly evidence itself to be the Word of God; yet, notwithstanding . . ." (*The Constitution of the United Presbyterian Church in the United States of America, Part I, Book of Confessions* [Philadelphia: 1967], 6.005).

"The Confession of the Waldenses" (1655) picked up several of these same marks, rightly focusing on the *teaching* of Scripture as the evidence of its inspiration: "We acknowledge the divinity of these sacred books, not only from the testimony of the Church, but more especially because of the eternal and indubitable truth of the doctrine therein contained, and of that most divine excellency, sublimity, and majesty which appears therein; and because of the operation of the Holy Spirit, who causes us to receive with reverence the testimony of the Church in that point, who opens our eyes to discover the beams of that celestial light which shines in the Scriptures . . ." (in Schaff, *Creeds,* 3:758).

Some have interpreted two phrases from this statement in support of the Hodge-Warfield approach to inerrancy, *viz.* "the consent of all the parts" and "the entire perfection thereof" (e.g., Lindsell, *Battle for the Bible,* p. 63). However, Jack Rogers, *Scripture in the Westminster Confession* (Grand Rapids: Zondervan, 1967) has shown that the types of apologetic and philosophical concerns which shaped the teaching of the Old Princeton theologians were not present in the deliberations of the Westminster divines. The "consent of all the parts" surely meant the doctrinal harmony of Scripture, while "the entire perfection thereof" affirmed that Scripture in its message and power was fully sufficient for all that God intended it to do.

9. ". . . this God reveals himself to men; firstly, in his works. . . . Secondly, and more clearly, in his Word, which was in the beginning revealed through oracles, and which was afterward committed to writing in . . . the Holy Scriptures" ("The French Confession of Faith" [A.D. 1559], Schaff, *Creeds,* 3:360).

10. Carl F. H. Henry's sentence concerning the dangers of Harold Lindsell's apologetic approach may be salient here: "A Bible unencumbered with some of his theories and standing on its own invulnerable supports, may be far more powerful than one propped up by retaining walls engineered by resolute evangelicals" (*New Review of Books and Religion,* September 1976, p. 7).

11. "We believe that the Word contained in these books has proceeded from God, and receives its authority from him alone, and not from men. And inasmuch as it is the rule of all truth, containing all that is necessary for the service of God and for our salvation, it is not lawful for men, nor even for angels to add to it, to take away from it, or to change it" ("The French Confession of Faith," Schaff, *Creeds,* 3:362).

12. For example, in Harold Lindsell's effort to show that the Bible preserves the mathematical value of *pi* in the dimensions of the molten sea (*Battle for the Bible,* pp. 165–66). Even Carl Henry, whose balanced perspective on the current debate has proved so helpful, has overplayed the inerrancy versus non-inerrancy theme. We can hope that in future discussions he will be more sensitive to the deeper issues of theological methodology and definition of inerrancy which underlie the present confusion. Cf. "Agenda for Evangelical Advance," *Christianity Today,* November 5, 1976, p. 38.

13. The recent interplay between Harold Lindsell and Robert Mounce illustrates my point that the key issue among evangelicals is not errancy or inerrancy, but what do we mean by error? Lindsell baits Mounce in a letter to *Eternity* (November 1976, p. 96): "Let Dr. Mounce say clearly that he believes that 'the Bible is free from all error in the whole and in the part' or let him say he believes there are some errors, however few, in the Bible." Mounce, perceptive theologian that he is, refuses to bite: "The Bible is without error in whole and in part. The controversy is over what constitutes an error."

14. "But we hold that interpretation of the Scriptures to be orthodox and genuine which is gleaned from the Scriptures themselves (from the nature of the language in which they were written, likewise according to the circumstances in which they were set down, and expounded in the light of like and unlike passages and of many and clearer passages) and which agree with the rule of faith and love, and contributes much to the glory of God and man's salvation"

("The Second Helvetic Confession" [A.D. 1566], *The Constitution of the United Presbyterian Church, Part I, Book of Confessions,* 5.010).

15. From Schaff, *Creeds,* 3:388.

16. E.g., Article VII of "The Thirty-Nine Articles of the Church of England" in Schaff, *Creeds,* 3:492: "Although the lawes geuen from God by Moses, as touchyng ceremonies and rites, do not bynde Christian men, nor the ciulle preceptes thereof, ought of necessitie to be receaued in any common wealth: yet not withstandyng, no Christian man whatsoeuer, is free from the obedience of the commaundementes, which are called morall."

17. Surely one of the better evangelical statements is that of the Lausanne Covenant (1974). It includes most of the great Reformation themes, while acknowledging the power of the Word to speak in all cultures. One of its strengths is that it leaves open the definition of "error": "We affirm the divine inspiration, truthfulness and authority of both Old and New Testament Scriptures in their entirety as the only written Word of God, without error in all that it affirms, and the only infallible rule of faith and practice. We also affirm the power of God's Word to accomplish his purpose of salvation. The message of the Bible is addressed to all mankind. For God's revelation in Christ and in Scripture is unchangeable. Through it the Holy Spirit still speaks today. He illumines the minds of God's people in every culture to perceive its truth freshly through their own eyes and thus discloses to the whole church ever more of the many-colored wisdom of God."